IMPASSIONED

A GUIDE TO PROGRESSIVE PREACHING

LUCAS HERGERT

SKINNER HOUSE BOOKS
BOSTON

 Published by Skinner House Books, an imprint of the Unitarian Universalist Association, 24 Farnsworth St., Boston, MA 02210–1409.

www.skinnerhouse.org

Printed in the United States

Cover design by Jeenee Lee
Text design by Tim Holtz

print ISBN: 978-1-55896-971-1
eBook ISBN: 978-1-55896-972-8

6 5 4 3 2 1
29 28 27 26 25

Cataloging-in-Publication information on file with the Library of Congress.

CONTENTS

INTRODUCTION

"My favorite thing is when you get us to *feel something*!" This was the exuberant Sunday-morning greeting of Mary "Chilli" Barlow, one of my congregation members. She was in her late eighties when she uttered those words, and I have not forgotten them. Even years later, after her death, her words remain a guidepost for my sermons. They constitute better advice than much of what is set down by mentors, colleagues, and preaching manuals. So simple: Get people to *feel something*. So simple, and yet so . . . challenging. Really, how does the preacher ensure the congregation not only receives but also feels the message?

Most preachers know Chilli's words contain valuable insight. Done well, preaching engages mind and heart, soul and body. It lures people into a world of felt experience. Unfortunately, worship and preaching become solely intellectual affairs all too often. This may happen because of the preacher's training or upbringing, neither of which made room for passion. Religious leaders may not know how to express themselves with feeling and power. In other cases, leaders may feel that passionate, emotional sermons are perfectly authentic and suitable to their style, but they find themselves preaching to unreceptive congregations. For them, shifting a resistant culture can be perplexing and frustrating. Whatever the reason, clergy may lack the resources to achieve a more passionate, embodied preaching experience. The book you hold seeks to change that.

A lack of resources does not equate to a lack of interest. Many are eager to learn how to preach with passion. My friend Robbie is a good example of this. He is a seminary student preparing for ministry with the Episcopal Church. I met him through an interfaith event, and one Sunday, he decided to attend my congregation on what happened to be Earth Day. I chose to preach on a text about creation from Genesis, linking it with our obligations to the natural world. I felt good about the service. After it came to an end, I was especially keen to welcome Robbie and thank him for coming. He greeted me with a hug and then asked enthusiastically, "How did you do that?" At first I wasn't sure what he meant, but he quickly elaborated, "None of my preaching mentors or professors discuss how to preach with that kind of passion. It was in your whole body. It vibrated through the whole space. How did you learn to do that?"

The truth is, I didn't always preach that way, nor was it modeled for me. I serve a Unitarian Universalist congregation and grew up in that tradition. This is a progressive denomination rooted in the Christian tradition and inclusive of multiple spiritual paths. Like many other mainline and progressive communities, the emotional temperature of the services is often kept low. Sermons are frequently thoughtful expositions rather than embodied, passionate events.

The first time I noticed this, I was twenty years old and sitting with my young-adult group in a church basement. I had recently made friends with a young woman new to the church. She was thrilled to find a congregation that had progressive values. Indeed, until she found our church, she hadn't known such a place existed. Having grown up in a conservative Evangelical home, she quickly came to love our church's theological openness and commitment to social justice—but she wondered about the emotional tone of the services. Her Evangelical roots included emotionally expressive worship, which meant praise music, heartfelt testimonies, and fiery sermons. More than anything else, she found it curious that we did not incorporate more emotional depth into the worship experience. In that young-adult meeting, she put it this way: "Sometimes I wonder if we are committed to our values. We can sound so intellectual—even theoretical—about them. I just wonder why we don't have more fire on Sundays."

Her question stuck with me. As I continued through my ministry training and found little to no information on how to preach with passion in my Unitarian Universalist context, I started to wonder if it was even possible to learn. Why were so many mainline and progressive congregations less expressive, embodied, emotional, and passionate? There seemed to be multiple barriers to doing so, both in the congregation and within my own approach to crafting sermons. It felt daunting, and indeed it was. Preaching with greater passion and emotional depth is no casual affair; it entails changing the way one selects topics, structures the sermon, understands the centrality of emotion, and attends to embodiment and delivery. It may also require changing the culture of a congregation that does not expect such animation. Many challenges arise when preachers attempt passionate expression.

Why take on these challenges? The reason is simple: Passionate preaching is powerful. It communicates one's emotional attachments to issues and values. Passionate preaching offers more than discussion about topics held at a distance; it claims a stake in them. Done well, it invites folks to experience a felt commitment to values that is both engaging and effective. As goes the apocryphal quotation attributed to Maya Angelou, "At the end of the day, people won't remember what you said or did, they will remember how you made them feel." By touching an emotional center, we enter a moment with the fullness of our hearts, bodies, and minds. The message registers at multiple levels of experience; it resonates deeply and is hard to dislodge. This kind of experience produces felt conviction that leads people to change their lives and social contexts.

I am especially interested in helping progressive clergy learn to preach with passion if it is not a part of their tradition. Despite the prevalence of conservative representation in politics and media, a vibrant tradition of religious progressivism persists in the US, extending back to abolitionists, suffragists, civil rights advocates, and peace activists. This religious progressivism includes people working for LGBTQ+ protections and equal marriage; it contains antiracists, environmentalists, and death-penalty abolitionists. It folds in luminaries such as Dorothy Day, Martin Luther King Jr., Sister Simone Campbell, and Cornel West. It follows the faithful critiques of feminist, liberationist, and queer theology. It is represented by individuals and communities within a wide range of denominations and religious traditions, including the voices of socialist Rabbi Michael Lerner, antiapartheid Muslim scholar Farid Esack, and peace activist and Buddhist monk Thich Nhat Hanh. Today, this tradition is embodied in the progressive Evangelicalism of Jim Wallis and *Sojourners*, the liberation theologians and liberal approaches in Catholicism, and the moral fusion politics of Rev. William Barber II and the Poor People's Campaign.

To be sure, these religious voices will not concur on all issues, nor will they necessarily claim the label of "progressive." Sometimes they will disagree heartily with each other. Instead of rigidly defining an in-group and out-group with this term "progressive," I find a big tent of faithful witnesses that share certain tendencies. They discover a common cause in movement and change—progress—for social betterment. They believe faith is at its best when it seeks justice for those who have been excluded. They challenge systems of domination that harm and degrade. And the taproot of their conviction is religious tradition. They draw deeply from diverse wells, including the life and teaching of Jesus of Nazareth, the prophets in the Hebrew scriptures, the language of the Qur'an, and the teachings of the Buddha, as well as other sources that challenge and motivate the hope for justice. It's a big project with a long history. And for it to continue, its good news needs passionate advocates. And preachers.

It's important to give credit where credit is due: Other traditions have achieved emotional heights with preaching. Evangelical pastors often preach with expression, passion, and power; their theories and practices of preaching hold a lot of wisdom. Alex Montoya is one such minister who has written about this. As he puts it in *Preaching with Passion*, "Our sermons need to come alive! They need to speak from the heart as well as from the head. They need to burn through our being and descend upon the lives of the hearers." While I find my theological and ethical positions quite far from those of Montoya, I can get behind his statement. The idea that preaching can (and should) ignite corners of the heart and touch depths of the human spirit resonates with my understanding and experience. What is more, many rhetorical techniques are portable if preachers are willing to reach outside of their comfort zones. Passionate preaching and speaking requires careful attention to one's own context and habits of expression, but anyone can learn. No tradition claims ownership; it cuts across culture, religion, politics, and class and appears in both sacred and secular arenas.

Any book on passion and preaching that fails to appreciate the contributions of the Black church isn't worth its salt. This tradition has not only mastered passionate oratory but its theorists also write about its dynamics, and I view their insights into preaching as invaluable. Some of my own teachers, Peter Gomes and Yvette Flunder, came from and are steeped in that tradition. The dozens of works on Black preaching that continue to grow each year are crucial companions for understanding passionate oratory—and yet, as Cleophus LaRue aptly puts it in "Two Ships Passing in the Night," white mainline and progressive preachers and the Black rhetorical tradition have too often failed to exchange insights. Cleophus LaRue, Rev. Henry Mitchell, and Frank Thomas are rightfully critical of preachers who ignore the wisdom of Black preaching, and I intend not to fall into that trap. This book hopes to acknowledge debts, lift voices, and foster respectful communication and exchange.

Other resources—religious and secular, artistic and dramatic, psychological and philosophical—will be used to offer techniques. There is such a variety of ways to think through embodiment and passion that, truly, it's too much to offer in a single work. And here's the thing: Learning to preach with passion is not about accepting a tidy set of tools from any one place. It is not about accepting or rejecting the "right way" to do it. Instead, it is about finding the practices and approaches that make sense to you, about locating the right techniques that will tug emotions up and out and ignite the heart and mind—which will mean something different depending on context, identity, and personal desire. This book will be successful if, in its pages, you locate some techniques that are effective for your unique voice, style, theology, and congregation.

I hold deep gratitude for preaching approaches that are not my own. At the same time, I recognize the perspective in this book is limited. I am writing from the viewpoint of a preacher trained in a predominantly white, middle-class, progressive denomination. This book aims to open the horizons of its preaching, broaden its intellectual resources, and challenge the limits of its emotional restraint. It is written with preachers in those particular contexts in mind, though I hope others will find wisdom within its pages. No doubt, there are other approaches to emotion and preaching that I have failed to consider, and I am certain my social location limits what I notice and fail to imagine. I do not intend for this book to give the final edict on this topic. Instead, I am excited to read preachers whose identities, passions, wisdom, and communities open further vistas.

Impassioned attempts three things: First, it is a practical guide to sermon preparation. It seeks to be a useful tool aimed at working clergy, busy seminary students, and interested lay leaders. In that spirit, the book shows readers how to construct a powerful sermon from start to finish. Readers who are relatively new to preaching will gain much practical advice.

Second, it provides seasoned preachers with a different angle on the craft. It is a guide for incorporating emotion into the language and structure of the sermon, as well as congregations that may not be receptive to it. Rethinking the sermon from the ground up frees preachers to offer a powerful, heartfelt word.

Finally, the book seeks to revitalize progressive sermons and ignite fiery preaching in cool sanctuaries. It shows preachers how to link passion with progressive commitments to create change in the lives of community members and their broader social context.

Each chapter gives preachers tools to accomplish these goals. Chapter 1 explores the history of passion in preaching, philosophical worries about emotion in speech giving, as well as the diverse ways the sermon can express passion. Chapter 2 turns to concerns over congregational norms, authenticity and preaching, and the preacher's identity. If you are not accustomed to preaching a passionate word, how might you do so in a way that remains authentic to your preaching voice while shifting emotional norms in the congregation? This chapter also discusses questions related to marginalized identities and emotional expression. Chapter 3 moves to the practical concerns of sermon crafting and offers the first two elements of the passionate sermon, including the interpretation of sacred texts and the use of empathy to discover the sermon's central message. Chapter 4 outlines the next two elements, which involve crafting language and determining the sermon structure that best aligns with emotional expression. Chapter 5 explores theories of communicating emotion through the body, acting strategies that facilitate passionate expression, and approaches to emotional crescendo in the sermon. Together, the topics covered in these chapters constitute the path to constructing a powerful, passionate preaching experience.

When Ralph Waldo Emerson reviewed some of his early lectures, he found them wanting. In *The Journals and Miscellaneous Notebooks of Ralph Waldo Emerson*, he writes that he discovered in them "fine things, pretty things, wise things." However, they contained "no arrows, no axes, no nectar, no growling, no transpiercing, no loving, no enchantment." His words were refined and well crafted, but they missed a vital and living element. To many preachers, his lament sounds familiar. How do we find more than pretty and wise things in our preaching? How do we locate the arrows and axes, the enchantment and nectar? How do we craft a sermon in a way that communicates the depth of our felt commitment to the issues we care for most? Some will say this is a natural inborn talent, one that cannot be taught. I beg to differ. Preaching with passion is a skill; it can be learned.

1

THE PATH TO PASSIONATE PREACHING

Sermons can fall flat. Most preachers have been there. I learned it the hard way early in my preaching career.

One warm winter day in California, I received news that hate speech had occurred in the community: The public menorah had been defaced with neo Nazi symbols. As I peered from my office window into the empty church parking lot, I pondered how I could speak to this issue. I knew members would come on Sunday, searching for a message that would sensitively respond to the city's worry and pain.

I spent a lot of time planning that message and response, more time than I usually spent on sermon preparation. Using contemporary stories and ancient verse, I argued for faithful solidarity against hate. I then proceeded to send that manuscript to a few close colleagues. Was I missing anything? Was the argument sound? Did they understand my point? Was there anything that didn't fit? While my friends offered some constructive advice, I consistently received positive feedback. It wasn't going to win a Pulitzer, but the ideas were sturdy.

That Sunday morning, I stood in my church's simple wooden pulpit. I grasped the light brown wood and searched the faces of my beloved congregation, the members of which had come to find a good word from their minister. The manuscript sat before me, prepared, polished, and rehearsed. I took a breath and began.

I carefully enunciated the main points; my voice and delivery were even and clear. As with most sermons I preach, I felt as though my time in the pulpit went quickly. I gave the last words and sat.

And that was when I knew it. My overriding thought was, *That didn't work.* And I had no idea why.

Of course, the failure of my sermon paled in comparison with the event it addressed. In a way, it didn't matter what I did or did not say. What mattered was the harm perpetrated in the community, and what could be done to address it. But as someone who cares deeply for the people I serve and who wishes to do better by them, I wanted to know why my sermon caved in. It didn't make sense. The ideas were well crafted. The delivery was poised. No earthquake disrupted the flow of the homily. There seemed to be nothing that prevented my sermon from doing what it needed to do. But it felt inadequate to the task.

My feeling was confirmed during the social hour afterward. A newer member of the congregation came up and hugged me, then said, "That was really nice. What do you call that, a talk? It was good." While intended as a compliment, I could not help but read into her words the problem I felt. A talk, such as a TED Talk, is a secular form of speech intended to communicate ideas. In contrast, a sermon is meant to communicate to the heart about life and values.

What was worse, I knew preachers who, when they offered a sermon, would never confuse it with another form of communication. You left their sermons feeling *preached to.* My sermon, by contrast, may have left folks with some good ideas and a positive message by affirming community solidarity. But I doubt anyone would have said they felt *preached to*. I doubt they left feeling much of anything.

I thought back to my friend Emily's words all those years earlier: "I just wonder why we don't have more fire on Sundays." She was onto something. Why were my words, despite being finely crafted, lacking in emotional resonance? Why had passion slipped past me? This would not be the last time I wondered this. As other events and occasions passed, I found myself without the tools to preach differently.

Such concerns plagued me as I listened to the sermons of other preachers. I was especially drawn to recordings of those who spoke with power and passion in the pulpit. From Evangelical ministers to preachers in the Black church tradition to highly effective secular speakers on progressive issues—I was wowed by their style. They expressed a full emotional range, from grief and lament to joy and outrage. Their language was full of feeling. And even though I was not physically in the congregation, I felt moved by their words—which only exaggerated my dissatisfaction. It seemed that preaching with passion was beautiful but foreign, something inaccessible to me.

I didn't feel that way in all contexts. In many parts of my life, I could express emotions that were authentic and true for me. Other communities I was a part of exhibited creativity and aliveness and showed models for expressing grief, outrage, pain, joy, and hope. But every time I got in the pulpit, I felt like I had to button up my collar the rest of the way. Fuller passionate and emotional expression was inaccessible, and so whenever I heard someone preach with conviction and passion, I would think, *It's a shame I can't do that.*

Until I didn't.

One evening, after feeling especially alive from listening to another sermon, I had a different thought. *What if I just started doing it?*

Easier said than done, I suppose. It took me quite some time—and a doctor of ministry in preaching to boot—to get there. My journey to passionate preaching required rethinking the emotional dynamics of preaching and reshaping the sermon in fundamental ways.

When I think about how I organized that early sermon versus how I organize sermons today, I see the distance traversed. Early on,

I started with an idea and then decided how to organize it. I found stories that helped support the idea and then led the gathered community to a conclusion. In this approach, emotion was treated as an unexpected and sporadic visitor, popping in at haphazard moments.

Today, I start by asking: What am I feeling about this event that happened in the world? Where does the emotion sit in my body? How can my words help communicate the felt experience? After I answer those questions, I develop ideas and stories that engage the emotional encounter. I then work on embodying the emotion in my delivery of the words—a fundamental change that leads to a very different result from how I was initially taught to preach.

And then there were the twists, turns, and obstacles along the way. While many enthusiastically welcomed greater emotional expression, others did not care for the change. I had to carefully consider the evolution of my preaching style in a denominational context that expected restraint. Skillfully navigating expectations was as important as the practical details of how to preach with passion.

This book is a map for the journey, aiming to reduce detours and false starts and help preachers get there faster than I did. It offers a clear guide for transforming the sermon into a passionate experience and event. And while it takes work, the destination is worth it. Engaging folks beyond intellect alone is a powerful thing, offering a fuller experience that connects the head and heart. And it is especially powerful for progressive preachers called to engage the issues that matter. Passionate preaching may not be a panacea for the challenges of religion in the twenty-first century. Nonetheless, it's a compelling alternative to the way sermons are preached in many mainline and progressive denominations. Effective use of passion changes the way the sermon is received by becoming so much more than an intellectual exercise, and people notice.

After all, no one in recent years has asked me whether my sermon was called a talk. Instead, people feel *preached to.*

A Brief History of Passion in Preaching

"The best lack all conviction, while the worst / Are full of passionate intensity." So writes William Butler Yeats in his chilling yet well-loved poem "The Second Coming." Each person will think of something different when they encounter the phrase *passionate preaching*. For some—perhaps many—this thought carries negative associations. Those people might imagine a speech from a troubling figure such as the 1970s cult leader Jim Jones. No doubt, passion in public oratory can be used for destructive and troubling ends. When someone with malevolent or misguided intentions holds an audience in thrall, the results can be disastrous; there is a long history of crowds swayed to dangerous or unsavory action through the manipulation of emotion. This causes many, especially those on the progressive side of the religious and political spectrum, to express discomfort with its rhetorical uses.

But does passionate preaching always or often lead to bad outcomes?

The word *passion* itself clues us into the wariness toward emotions in speech giving. It goes back to the Greek *pathos*, meaning "to feel," "to suffer," "to experience," and "to undergo." When emotions arise, we often find ourselves given over to them whether or not we like it. They come with urgency and heat, which worries philosophers who value the cool distance of reason and cause many to dismiss emotions as unreliable reactions. In this view, emotions motivate us to act out of our right minds. Like a gust of wind that pushes us from a ledge, there is no intelligence to them.

Often, these philosophers treat emotions as arising from instinct, a primal or atavistic part of ourselves. Roman philosopher Seneca, for instance, likened emotions to fire, fierce winds, ocean currents, and intruding forces that threatened to cut up and dismember the self. "Anger," Seneca writes in *On Anger*, "tramples self-restraint underfoot, steeps its hands in slaughter, scatters abroad the limbs of its children." In other words, he viewed emotions as erratic impulses that need to be restrained and diminished.

Many philosophers think this view is bunk. They argue that emotion possesses its own kind of intelligence—that it is a sophisticated interaction with our environments, which, in turn, informs our responses. The view of emotions as intelligent also has ancient roots, beginning with Aristotle. In the *Nicomachean Ethics*, he argues that experiencing the right emotion, to the right degree, toward the right object, is essential for being human. In contrast to Seneca, Aristotle thought anger, as well as other emotions, could be appropriate, motivating, and helpful. Indeed, people lacked something essential when they encountered gross injustice and felt no anger; they were, in his estimation, "foolish," according to the *Nicomachean Ethics*. Similarly, someone who eradicates their emotional responses diminishes a part of their humanity; emotions should be considered rather than feared or neglected. Anger offers information about injustice and encourages corrective action. The wise nurture and attend to such emotions while moderating excesses.

Many modern philosophers agree. They, too, reject the view of emotions as merely erratic or dangerous impulses and argue that emotions possess intelligence, directing us to pursue the good and reject what is harmful. In Martha Nussbaum's *Upheavals of Thought*, she says, "Emotions have to do with whatever I do value, however well or badly those things fit together." Emotions are not blunt sensations; rather, they are tied to and responsive to the things human beings cherish. Emotions do not arrive as mysterious, implacable forces but as complex evaluations of our environments and conditions; they sensitively gauge the texture of our circumstances.

For instance, sorrow not only responds to loss but also judges the severity of it. Minor regret is different from true grief; I am unlikely to experience the latter because of a misplaced cell phone. Rather, severe grief is likely to occur when I lose someone I dearly love. Of course, we do not always get the memo—the cause of our emotional response is sometimes opaque. But emotion is often carefully attuned to circumstance while organizing our lives toward cherished values and ends.

One public concern about emotion in speech giving is that it manipulates. People get "whipped up" and "act out of their right minds." Unscrupulous speakers use emotion to push people around against their better judgment. At the same time, we underestimate the intelligence of emotions—and people—when we assume a passionate speech will cause them to readily violate their core convictions. In *Celebration and Experience in Preaching*, preaching scholar Henry Mitchell reports once having heard "a whole congregation of habitual shouters suddenly and rationally wax silent" when a preacher violated the community's core theological understandings. I have witnessed similar emotional withdrawals in crowds, which lends further credence to the idea that emotions include or are tied to an intelligent evaluative capacity. This does not change the fact that crowds sometimes give themselves over to harsh feelings and bad reasons, but it is worth pondering what quiet habits of hatred were cultivated long before they were provoked by a speech. Passionate speech that incites violence likely plays on embedded prejudice—in other words, members of the crowd may concur with the speech and speaker long before they gather.

The power of emotions can motivate as well as evaluate, providing information about how one should understand and act within the world. They get us off the couch and make us move. Emotions can make us change behaviors in a relationship, prevent a dangerous choice, incite care for those within and outside our immediate presence, and organize us for political activity. They can inspire us to pursue what we value and care for. Such motivation applies not only to personal projects but to public undertakings. When I value a political goal, such as antiracism, I feel some degree of passionate attachment to the achievement of racial justice. Without working toward and achieving that concept of justice, I feel frustration or guilt. These feelings motivate me to continue the pursuit. Though emotions can misfire, mislead, and be manipulated, and though we may be motivated to pursue bad ends, emotions motivate action, and that action can be in pursuit of worthy goals.

So, it cannot be that only "the worst are filled with passionate intensity." Passionate speech, or speech that touches emotions, cannot only be the domain of the ethically unsavory. When people are asked, "What's the first thing that pops into your head when you encounter the phrase *passionate speech*?" many give the same answer: Dr. Martin Luther King Jr.'s "I Have a Dream" speech. Everything about that speech—its cadence, rhythm, timing, structure, use of pace and silence, crescendo, and response to the audience—is a master class in passionate oratory. It was designed and delivered to create an emotional response. And it's clear that King was tapping emotion and passion to motivate specific actions: He was calling on Congress to pass federal legislation outlawing segregation and encouraging everyday folks to pressure legislators until that happened.

For King, the effectiveness of the sermon was as much about its passion as its reason, its pathos as well as its logos. Steeped within the traditions of the Black church, he intuitively and intellectually understood the effectiveness of emotional oratory. It was fuel to sustain the community and motivate action. King knew that without the use of emotion in speech giving, the preacher may lack the force to inspire. The preacher may believe the argument of a sermon is well crafted and offers persuasive reasons to care about an issue, and yet, the community will not only—or even primarily—ask, "Are these reasons sound and valid?" Instead, members will also wonder, "Do I feel sufficiently motivated to act on behalf of these values?"

If the preacher supplies reasons but fails to provide compelling emotional force, the sermon may write checks from an empty account. This was the issue with the sermon I preached at the beginning of my ministry, the one about the instance of hate speech. It was well reasoned but lacked emotional force. Without passion, the words fell flat.

A significant part of white mainline and progressive preaching has resisted emotional expression in the pulpit. This resistance goes beyond simple anxiety about emotional manipulation in speech giving. Historians and sociologists offer different theories about this development. Potential influences include the creation and differentiation of the white middle class as having distinctive habits of reticence and reserve, the early American established churches' rejection of the Great Awakening and its fiery preaching style, and religion's bid for legitimacy amid the rise of scientific values of objectivity and distance. Philosopher James K. A. Smith offers a theoretical explanation of the Enlightenment's emphasis on rationality and its influence on religious groups, which saw humans as primarily thinking beings who needed to be persuaded with reason. In *Desiring the Kingdom*, Smith memorably describes this line of thinking as "so fixated on the cognitive that it assumes a picture of human beings that look like bobbleheads: mammoth heads that dwarf an almost nonexistent body" and argues that this distorted anthropology continues to shape the texture of many worship practices. It ignores embodiment and the emotional capacities of the gathered community while overinvesting in the rational faculties, framing worship as a time for edifying the mind while neglecting the heart.

For many communities and preachers, such emotional neutrality has become the norm. This reality has impacted homiletic content and form, privileging intellectual argument and exploration. Sermons are organized around creedal matters to be taught, theological propositions to be debated, and scriptural meanings to be disputed. Adherents write sermons with a structure similar to a standard essay, where a proposition or thesis is backed up with supporting points. Preachers prefer language that communicates a message in simple, clear, and straightforward ways, treating poetry and narrative as inferior vehicles for truth. Many manuals call poems and stories "illustrations" of the sermon's thesis, implying their redundancy and superfluity and reducing them to the dessert that made the main course palatable.

This has been a tough set of habits for preachers to break; it endured in many mainline and progressive denominations until the late twentieth century. As recently as the 1980s, David Rankin wrote in "From the Masthead to the Hatches," "Probably the most prevalent model of preaching within the liberal churches is that of the college professor lecturing to a class of students." Let that sink in.

Obviously, both the speculative theologian and the professorial preacher gave priority to reason and rational argument and had little use for emotion or passion. Abstractions and ideas took up residence in the house of mainline homiletics. Emotions and passion, meanwhile, were relegated to the servants' quarters. This trend persisted despite the occasional arrival of florid language and sentimental pulpit styles.

Preaching has evolved. Indeed, Rankin wrote those words at a pivotal juncture in the development of mainline homiletic theory. The 1970s and 1980s were a time of deep questioning in the field, an era when new ways of conceiving the sermon were developed. The inductive and narrative sermon forms were representative of this trend and organized around "images, stories, and scenes rather than on the logic of argument," as Eunjoo Mary Kim writes in *The Renewed Homiletic*. Instead of presenting hard-drawn conclusions that were then backed up with evidence, sermons in these forms invited members to follow the preacher on a path of discovery. A conclusion emerged only at the end and was issued as an invitation rather than a declaration. The point was to facilitate an experience of faith, not to argue someone into agreement on a point.

Careful research for preaching preparation was still necessary, but this method's experiential emphasis alleviated the demand for obvious professorial flexing. Neither new learning nor intellectual assent was the main purpose. (Indeed, some argue that the ratio of new information should remain relatively low because the sermon is meant to remind people of the values they already have, rather than argue for the adoption of unfamiliar concepts.)

This approach to preaching was a breath of fresh air. Deflating some of the headiness of the earlier forms made room for a more emotionally satisfying experience. And yet there was still a missing piece, even with inductive and narrative sermon theories—both of which often failed to mention the role of emotion in sermon crafting and preaching explicitly.

For instance, Fred Craddock's *As One Without Authority* and Eugene Lowry's *The Homiletical Plot*, both pivotal for the changing mainline and progressive homiletic landscape, spent relatively little time on delivery and emotion. Indeed, sermons in this mold opened new horizons for preaching and invited greater appreciation for how folks engaged with the homily. And yet this move was no guarantor of passionate delivery.

From a practical perspective, this isn't a shock. Without an explicit focus on facilitating emotion, feelings may not come across. One can, for instance, recite a well-crafted poem about joy without necessarily expressing the emotion. It's a little like mixing all of the ingredients together and then not being sure how to turn on the oven.

Of course, some traditions turn up the heat. Many preachers in the Black church tradition are carefully attuned to the emotional dynamics of a sermon. Often beginning with lament and ending with celebration, their sermons are crafted as an experience of embodied passion. Henry Mitchell is the preeminent theorist of the form; Rev. Martin Luther King Jr., Rev. Gardner C. Taylor, Prathia Hall, Rev. Dr. Otis Moss III, and Rev. James Forbes are only a few of the recent torchbearers. Unfortunately, preaching theory and preachers from predominantly white traditions have often failed to appreciate these contributions. As William C. Turner writes in "The Musicality of Black Preaching," "Historically, detractors of black preaching have misunderstood the dynamics and devalued the form as being overly emotional and devoid of reason and theological value." Despite the tomes explaining and commending the theological and rhetorical significance of the form, many in predominantly white traditions have simply ignored its genius.

The same is true for Evangelical preaching, though the reasons are different. The theological and political gulf between progressive congregations and many Evangelical communities is deep and wide, a chasm that was cut at the time of the Great Awakening and has stayed intact. In fact, the expressive diversity is sometimes used as shorthand for the theological differences. Just as different cultural spaces have distinct modes of behavior and communicative styles, some characterize detached intellectual presentation and embodied passionate expression as belonging only to certain communities. They might even call passionate preaching "the Evangelical style." But this understanding is limited for multiple reasons. I have witnessed deep and authentic passionate expression in progressive contexts; likewise, Evangelical preachers such as Jim Wallis and Rob Bell offer brilliant and insightful messages. What's more, this stereotype often implies that a preacher can appeal either to intellect or to emotion, but not both. Such thinking ignores not only the reality that reason and passion can be brought together but also the many techniques available to do so.

The use of passionate expression within traditions is complex. Traditions are not monolithic; rather, they are rich, vast, and varied.

They have their own debates about what constitutes skillful expression and why passion is important (or not). Indeed, Jerry Vines and Adam Dooley wrote *Passion in the Pulpit* because they believe the Evangelical church is losing its capacity to effectively express passion, which they attribute to several factors, including a misunderstanding of what passion entails. Many equate passion with excessive loudness and vigorous gesture, and preachers either lean into that or flee. Vines and Dooley attempt to reframe emotion and passion for the Evangelical pulpit, offering methods of interpreting the emotion of scripture and thoughtfully crafting it in the sermon. Likewise, Cleophus J. LaRue wrote *Rethinking Celebration* as a critique of passionate celebration in the Black church. Too much emphasis on that element can lead, he writes, to a shallow festivity that washes out the transformative intentions of the sermon and can exclude powerful sermons delivered in a quieter voice. He argues instead for a theory of worship that engages multiple forms and attends to the theological and behavioral intentions of the sermon.

In other words, the dynamics of passionate pulpit styles are often renegotiated from within the communities that house them. Passionate preaching is not (and shouldn't be) a matter of cutting and pasting from another community, which too often degenerates into a caricature that fails to do justice to complex traditions. There is neither one way to do it nor consensus about how it should be done, no one tradition to borrow from nor a ready-made set of skills that can slide from one pulpit to the next. Instead, to effectively use passion, one must carefully consider what will facilitate and hinder emotion, which entails careful reflection on the ways one experiences and expresses emotions and necessitates a deep understanding of one's context, body, voice, language, and theology. In addition to considering which tools are effective and which ones aren't, preachers must consider what will be effective for *them.* Only when these elements are appreciated in their fullness and complexity can passion flourish.

Historically, preaching has always made use of tools and techniques of the broader culture. For instance, many early Christian preachers were trained in classical rhetoric (which, incidentally, gave significant attention to the use of pathos in speech giving.) Later, Enlightenment philosophy, African rhythms, scientific discourse, novels, radio, and television impacted the form of address. In recent decades, homiletics scholars have only broadened the imagination of what preaching could become. Many have asked, How would the sermon change if its scenes were conceptualized like a movie or television show? How would it change if it were structured like improv or jazz? What about using the tools of poetry and creative nonfiction?

It doesn't take much imagination to push this a little bit further and imagine opening elements of delivery in the same way. What if, for instance, preachers thought about the expression of emotion in the pulpit through the lens of acting techniques? What if preachers crafted the sermon in the same way that a singer crafts the emotional arc of a song? What if preaching availed itself of psychological theories of embodiment and emotional transmission? The consideration of approaches to preaching from outside of homiletics is fertile soil for understanding and cultivating passion. There are models available that anticipate dynamic emotional engagement, which can impact sermon delivery. These examples offer rich possibilities for thinking about what can bring preaching alive.

Is preaching alive today? And is preaching bringing people alive today? Many sermons structured and delivered to appeal to intellect alone are unable to touch the depths of human experience. They are stuck in a distorted anthropology and homiletic theory that misses a crucial affective dimension of the human experience. What if preaching started with the questions: What will make the heart quicken? What will tap emotions that are deep and true? How can I find the courage and capacity to express what makes me come alive?

In *Queer Soul and Queer Theology*, theologians Laurel C. Schneider and Thelathia "Nikki" Young write, "Living is what happens when one is able to feel, connect, desire, enjoy, and flourish in one's embodied existence—in one's skin and nerves, breath and bones." That, to me, is the heart of passionate preaching, an invitation to inhabit the fullness of the human experience—body, emotion, and intellect—in the pulpit and beyond. It celebrates and lives in our embodied selves, touching emotion, passion, and fire. Why would we settle for anything less? Why would we tolerate worship that forbids, ignores, or denies this?

That's just the thing: I don't think we have to.

Aligning Logos with Pathos

The Latin root of the word *preach* is *proclaim*. Throughout history, the sermon has served as a key practice for proclaiming a community's convictions: It restates, refines, and develops the commitments of the congregation and faith tradition, and it names religious values and inspires people to live by them. Of course, one can overstate the inspirational power of the sermon. The idea that the preacher proclaims a message and the congregation mechanically follows it is simplistic and unrealistic. This view can lead preachers to believe they possess unwarranted power. Moreover, it removes the capacity for freedom and the complexities of discernment from the lives of members. Nonetheless, there is a force within the sermon, one that can shape and reshape consciousness. It plants seeds that sprout in unexpected ways.

An example of this is a sermon I preached about a year ago. Within a larger message about environmental care, I described the pain of seeing a ravine I had played in as a child filled with construction waste. The next Sunday, a member of my community told me I had almost gotten her arrested. Surprised and somewhat disturbed, I asked her why. She said she was trying to pick up garbage along a street near her home, which turned out to be private property. An officer rolled up to ask her what was going on. "I'm just doing what my pastor said!" she told the officer. Apparently charmed, he let her walk away with only a warning.

When I am listing intentions for my sermons, getting members arrested for picking up trash is not high on the list. But this story reminds me that words have power and can leave a lasting impression.

When one crafts a sermon that resonates on a deep emotional level, it inspires people to change their lives and world. Not even the most skillful passionate preachers can totally plan for this to happen; sometimes it happens independently of the preacher's intentions. However, there are methods one can use to craft an effective sermon that has a lasting impact, which requires the successful alignment of the sermon's rational intention with emotional force. The fancy language for this—what's used in the discipline of rhetoric—is that it joins together logos with pathos. When these component parts align, one has the makings of a passionate sermon.

Hence, I define passionate preaching as the intentional alignment of the sermon's logic (logos) with the emotional experience and expression (pathos) of the preacher and receivers such that it produces a purposeful change.

This definition resists two common views of passion and emotion in preaching, the first of which is what I call the "get loud here" definition: the idea that passionate expression means the preacher will start shouting their message. While this concept of passion in preaching predominates, it lacks both nuance and effectiveness. Rhythm, pace, silence, cadence, intonation—all of these are considerations that impact passionate expression. Moreover, depending on the emotional structure of the sermon, a quiet delivery might be more appropriate. The second view I resist is what I call the "shed tear here" idea of emotional preaching: the idea that emotional expression is limited to telling a sentimental story and getting choked up. Sure, effective use of emotion in preaching attends to pain and lament, but it must be organic to the message. Additionally, sermons may include the range of human emotional expression and consider the unique ways various emotions (sadness, wonder, tenderness, outrage, joy, etc.) are crafted in language and shown in delivery.

When the elements of pathos and logos are thoughtfully brought together, the sermon finds its propulsion. It moves. One feels compelled to journey with the preacher from beginning to end. There is a certain intangibility here, a complex dynamic that eludes precise description. Perhaps it is akin to the functioning of an engine. Without electricity, an engine is just a hunk of metal—an intricate hunk of metal, but not much more. When it finds its electric current, the engine suddenly whirs to life. So, too, with the sermon. Without a compelling emotional cause, the sermon is just a hunk of words. But when the preacher finds the emotional core and aligns it with language, structure, and delivery, this sparks the sermon's ignition. It electrifies the message, pulling others along for the ride.

Unfortunately, the emotional content of the sermon is sometimes treated like an extraneous or irrelevant flourish rather than its engine. When I was a kid, my teacher would reward us with stickers for good behavior. Because of the glue, the stickers would often peel off our shirts or backpacks. Many of us have experienced sermons where the emotions feel like those stickers: cheaply pasted on and quick to fall off.

For instance, a sermon that feels maudlin or sentimental may result from a message that does not warrant a story of heartbreak. People may feel their emotions are being "milked" by a story that is inessential to the message. Alternatively, a preacher may become excessively worked up when the message itself does not merit the response. Perhaps the preacher is shouting with the goal of communicating heightened emotion, but the language and message do not warrant such expression. In this case, folks may feel the sermon is much ado about nothing. To avoid these misfortunes, the preacher needs to understand how particular emotions function and then align them thoughtfully with language and delivery to ensure the emotion coheres to the structure of the message and doesn't peel off.

It would be interesting but difficult to list every conceivable emotion and then speculate on how they impact the preaching process. Creating such an exhaustive list would require a much longer tome—something the size of the Bible, perhaps, if such a book could even be written. Psychologists and philosophers disagree about the number of emotions and even what counts as an emotion. Aristotle, for instance, argued for fourteen emotions, including fear, confidence, anger, friendship, calm, enmity, shame, shamelessness, pity, kindness, envy, indignation, emulation, and contempt. Charles Darwin, in contrast, argued for a shorter list, possibly as few as five: fear, anger, sadness, happiness, and love. Later schools identify as many as twenty-seven, sometimes more. This does not even scratch the surface of cultural differences—both the controversial idea that some cultures possess emotions that other cultures do not, and the reality that some cultures name emotions others have no word for. Rather than create an exhaustive list, I will describe emotions frequently evoked in the pulpit. By exploring what these do, we can better align our sermon's message with an organic underlying emotional subtext. Attending to the structure, presentation, and alignment of these emotions will make the engine of the sermon hum.

Outrage or prophetic anger is a common emotion that flares in the pulpit and can be traced back to the Hebrew prophets, who decried injustice and railed against hoarded wealth. Some of the greatest preachers in recent times have used this emotion skillfully.

These sermons ask the community to care about the misalignment of how the world is and how the world ought to be—and seek to change it. They touch on genuine and legitimate feelings of rage and channel it against the dynamics of oppression. In *Womanist Ethics and the Cultural Production of Evil*, Emilie Townes eloquently frames the perspective of communities of color that struggle against racist tropes: "We must name ourselves with precise anger and ornery love while churning justice and truth into a new analysis of our ethical dilemma." This is a rage that doesn't flame out but rather burns for justice. It is clearly focused, directed, and resolute; it names oppressive realities and dares to imagine a different future.

The history of lament runs as deep as outrage with a similar origin. The Hebrew prophets often lamented when the Israelites turned away from the higher calling of justice, when their neighbors ignored the poor and dispossessed, and when faced with violence, war, and forced emigration. The purpose was not to wallow in sadness. Instead, it was an act of protest. In "Rending the Curtain," Robert C. Dykstra calls lament "vulnerable aggression," meaning that in feeling and empathizing with heartbreak and grief, one finds the courage to act against that which destroys and dehumanizes. Lament may ask members to mourn what has been lost, protest the loss, and prevent such loss in the future.

In the pulpit, it is often easier to tap into negative emotions than positive ones. There is something ephemeral about brighter emotions that makes them challenging to engage. As Naomi Shihab Nye puts it in her poem "So Much Happiness," "happiness floats." While we can reliably turn to situations that provoke heartbreak and rage, joy is less dependable; it can feel like a fickle, unreliable, and even superfluous emotion, like a rabbit that disappears inside the magician's hat—here one minute, gone the next. Perhaps this is also why, according to theologian Justin E. Crisp in *Joy and Human Flourishing*, contemporary scholarly theology has only infrequently addressed joy, despite the fact that joy has a deep history within religion, from Gospel stories to Sufi poetry to Hindu ethics.

Part of the worry over joy has to do with its relationship to human suffering. Too often, religious traditions use bright feelings such as joy to steamroll experiences of pain. In his 2015 book *Blue Note Preaching in a Post-Soul World,* Rev. Dr. Otis Moss III puts it this way: “America is living stormy Monday, but the pulpit is preaching happy Sunday.” This tendency has, in his words, left “severe ecclesiastical and theological side effects.” One of these side effects is the impression that a community’s joy must be indifferent and even callous to the suffering in the world. It is joy in the bunker, shut off from what is happening in the streets. But this outcome is not necessary or inevitable; joy can respond to the alleviation of pain and grief. When suffering is tended to and justice prevails, that, too, can provoke joy and serve as a motivating force for the good. When handled deftly, joy can smash through insularity and ask the community to rejoice in the good that relieves sorrow, pain, and oppression.

While little has been written about joy in formal theology, the same cannot be said for hope. It is a staple for preachers and theologians alike. When I was a student minister, I told my mentor I was not sure what a good first sermon would be, and he advised, “Preach on hope—it rarely fails.” While my views on hope and theology have changed considerably since that early sermon, I have continued to heed his advice.

Part of what makes hope compelling is the gulf between hope and optimism. Optimism thrives in sunny times; it points the way toward a future that is already arriving and, we are certain, will continue to come. Hope, by contrast, is nourished in desolate climes. It does better with uncertainty, with the lack of clarity that things will get better. Instead of looking toward the bright horizon, hope scours modest instances that glimmer with unrealized future possibilities, which is what makes it an ideal preaching companion. When evidence of progressive ideals is in short supply, hope illuminates and motivates future possibilities. It does not bolt down the future, explaining exactly how things will improve, nor does it insist people just look on the bright side and think good thoughts. But it stubbornly refuses to surrender possibility. José Esteban Muñoz, writing on LGBTQ+ oppression in the United States in *Cruising Utopia*, puts it this way: "The here and now is a prison house." Hope, he writes, "allows us to see and feel beyond the quagmire of the present." In this way, it allows one to dream a better reality and act for it even without certainty.

Love is another emotion that shows up frequently in the pulpit. But of all the emotions I have named, love is perhaps the vaguest. The love that one has for a parent or a child, for a romantic interest, and for humanity writ large are vastly different experiences. And yet in the English language, they are lumped together under one word, which is especially complicated when we consider the emotional tenor of each of those experiences. The felt experience of unconditional love for a child is different from the romance one feels for a partner; both are alien from the experience of the love for one's neighbor. The meaning of the concept is scattered not only by intellectuals who interpret it differently but by a linguistic multiplicity that seems unable to stabilize what, precisely, it signifies.

This is why some people try to limit love. They may, for instance, recoil from talk of love beyond romance and family. They argue that unconditional love or romantic enthusiasm are nonstarters when applied to public life. Kurt Vonnegut famously said that love was too strong a word for the day to day. But what these critics fail to notice is that love in a public sense resonates less on the level of sentimental attachment. Rather, it vibrates at the level of conviction. This is what I take Emilie Townes to mean when she writes of "ornery love." It is a love that finds itself in seeking justice; as she writes in

Womanist Ethics and the Cultural Production of Evil, "Love without justice is asking for trouble." When love is engaged as an emotion in the sermonic form, it is often this level of conviction that provides the felt subtext of the sermon. The wise preacher makes use of love as a conviction that facilitates the struggle for justice.

Now that we've explored the texture of some of the emotions commonly brought into the pulpit, it is important to appreciate their dialectical nature. Emotions often respond to and contain a trace of their lack or opposite. Thirteenth-century Sufi mystic Rumi stated this sentiment beautifully in his poem "Birdwings": "Your deepest presence is in every small contracting and expanding, the two as beautifully balanced and coordinated as birds' wings." We can witness this dialectic threaded through the emotional experiences named above. Like the open hand that contains the experience of its closing, the balance of its contraction and expansion, emotions point beyond their immediacy. Joy dances with sorrow just as hope dances with despair. Love responds to hate and indifference. Lament is an act of cherishing a good that was lost, while anger points us toward justice that was thwarted or frustrated.

This understanding is crucial for engaging emotions in the sermon-crafting process. The dynamism of preaching emerges not only from chiming single notes of emotional experience but by playing chords of contradiction and negation. For example, a sermon on joy without an exploration of sorrow may sound sentimental. A sermon on the pain of lament should surface the tenderness of love for what has been lost; without that, the sermon will plunge people into despair. A sermon on love should glimpse the context of indifference and hate in which people struggle. Effective sermons plumb the depths of psychological complexity. Often, the tension implicit in these contradictions sustains the energetic propulsion of the sermon; one plucks the notes of negative emotional experience in ways that make people yearn for resolution. The brighter emotion of the resolution is a nuanced response with a depth that will not soon be forgotten.

A sermon utilizes pathos as its organizing force by relying on tension generated by this dialectical process. We can think of this in relation to the sermon's most basic elements: a movement of words through time. To command attention during that span of time, the preacher must provoke tension; it is this tensive quality of the sermon that sustains interest. While tension can be curated by organizing ideas and theologies that contradict and clash, it can also be produced through emotional experience. An experience of despair that dances with hope will provoke tension, as will an experience of lament that interweaves with joy. The congregation will wonder how the preacher is going to encounter the despair or lament and offer new possibility. This does not mean that one dismisses or negates the honest despair, rage, or pain, all of which can be legitimate responses to injustice and precarity. But the skillful use of dialectics will offer some hope of presence, healing, and witnessing, even in situations of tragedy. It is this dialectical element that structures the sermon's pathos and commands the listener's interest.

Discovering the pathos happens alongside discovering the logos, which requires finding the compelling reason that will drive the sermon. Often, this message is fleshed out with story, anecdote, theology, and other resources. It is the intersection of this commanding purpose or message, threaded through with emotion, that produces the experience of passion. In other words, the congregation will not experience lament as a disembodied, general feeling. That would be akin to experiencing an emotion for no particular reason. Instead, those gathered will experience lament *about* something, *for* something, stitched into the language and reason of the preacher's words. They will experience it in a sermon about war, immigration, climate crisis, racism, homophobia, or wealth disparity because it is drawn in vivid language about particular people and scenarios. And if they experience the kernel of hope in the lament, that, too, is because it is stitched into the language and delivery of the sermon. It is only when logos and pathos are harmonized that the effect of the passionate sermon is achieved.

We will spend much more time on message, structure, and language in the coming chapters. But here we can pause and savor the reasons for preaching with passion and emotional depth. They connect us with our full being and experience, point us toward what we value, align the content of the sermon with appropriate felt expression, motivate change in our lives and world, produce a driving force for the sermon, and give the sermon gravity so that it is not forgotten. Of course, emotions are as complex as people; they also contain undesirable elements. But if you have lingering doubts about the validity of and need for passion, I hope this chapter has offered an alternative perspective. Emotions are deep parts of who we are and how we value, and preachers ignore them at their peril. Indeed, ignoring emotions risks making the sermon ignorable.

At this point, many preachers will begin to wonder how they might incorporate deeper emotional engagement into their sermons. This is partially a question of *how* can I craft a sermon that elicits a passionate response? But it is also a question of how can *I*? If one has never done this before, or if the congregation expects little emotional engagement, worries over congregational receptivity and personal authenticity abound. These concerns are only compounded by issues of emotional expression and embodiment by those with marginalized identities. When you first begin to incorporate emotion into your preaching, you might encounter fundamental obstacles, especially if passionate preaching conflicts with your congregation's norms and expectations. Without intention, the preacher's fire can burn out in cool sanctuaries.

2

FIERY SERMONS IN COOL SANCTUARIES

Belinda Subraman's poem "Book Passion" describes a dream in which she is sitting in a restaurant. But rather than eating a tasty meal, she cuts into a book. Others in the dream are reading their books as she eats hers. Apparently, it has the texture of watercress. The crowd starts to notice her strange delicacy, and she feels uncomfortable, but she keeps chewing. She realizes they cannot be satisfied: "Their eyes / would never make them full."

To preach with passion is to do a strange thing. It is to do something grittier and more embodied than polite, monotone discussion; it is to experience and deliver a message from the gut. Many denominational and congregational contexts—my own included—are unaccustomed to preaching with passion. It is historically anathema. In some contexts, preaching with passion is as strange as eating the sermon manuscript in front of people. When you start doing it, you will get some stares, and yet it can be a more nourishing way to preach. You begin to suspect the bloodless, emotionless sermon lacks nutrients for congregants. It will never make them full.

But how does one chew through these changes? Doing so is no casual affair. It means understanding how emotional norms—which often come couched in phrases like "we don't do that kind of thing here"—function in congregational life and how to navigate them. Further, depending on one's social location, passionate preaching will be received differently. People of different genders, races, and sexual orientations will confront unique challenges. This is especially true for the reception of emotional presentation, which is heavily mediated by the preacher's identity. Finally, a turn toward passionate preaching contends with questions of authenticity. If a preacher alters their style, they may encounter sentiments that suggest passionate preaching is not really for them. Such opinions from members and mentors encourage the preacher to keep with familiar styles and approaches.

It's a lot to chew on, but the passionate preacher needs to grapple with these issues if they are going to be effective. For those eager to get to the practical portion about sermon crafting, I invite you to hang in there. This section gives a fuller view of what it means to preach with passion and how to make the necessary shifts. It will be a helpful setup for when, in the next chapter, we start digesting the practical details.

Emotional Norms in the Congregation

Changing one's approach to preaching and worship means contending with cultural norms in the congregation. Attempts to shift these norms can be met with pushback.

Sociologists have developed a large body of work on social norms and the ways they regulate behavior. Experts define social norms as pervasive habits that extend to most facets of our lives and regulate dress, gender, etiquette, sexuality, social status, and racial and class hierarchies, among other things. These norms are often naturalized, meaning they are treated as the fate of the mature, healthy, moral person rather than as constructed or artificial expectations. People who behave differently, who break with the codes of social norms, are often perceived as outsiders. Sometimes these folks are excluded from participation in the community or are sanctioned and disciplined until they accommodate the norms. The pervasiveness of social norms means they are present not only in secular life but in sanctuaries as well. One must think carefully about the tools available to shift expectations if one is going to make a difference.

At first, it can be jarring to think of social norms in relation to emotions. Emotions are sometimes thought of as primal or raw, touching a core of the self that is impervious to social interference. Nonetheless, emotions, like other aspects of human life, are highly regulated by norms. One example of this is the exchange of gifts. An expression of indifference or disdain, even if that is true to the gift receiver's experience, would be deemed by many as socially deviant. Other examples of emotional nonconformity or deviance could include weeping openly on public transportation, displaying happiness about a friend's insolvency, shouting at a store clerk for failing to print a receipt, exhibiting gloominess at someone's birthday party, frequently expressing envy over a partner's social interactions, or directing anger toward one's boss. To be sure, it's possible to imagine some of these emotional expressions as acceptable in particular moments—you can, of course, complain about your boss to a friend, but doing so in the boardroom could lead to unhappy consequences. Where, why, and how one is permitted to express emotions is complex socially regulated terrain.

When I first began preaching with a greater emotional range, I worried about the congregation's existing norms. As with other social spaces, congregations have unspoken expectations about emotional expression; these are often highly regulated environments. It is no accident that in his 2015 book *An Invitation to the Sociology of Emotions*, author Scott R. Harris uses a church service to explore the concept of emotional norms. He writes:

> As a child attending Catholic mass at my local church, I remember looking around at all the somber faces and subdued voices. Prayers were uttered with a calm seriousness; hymns were sung in solemn tones. After ceremonies—on the church steps and sidewalk—my parents spoke in upbeat voices with their friends or the parents of my friends. But

> during mass, the emotional tenor was restrained. Even when parishioners were invited to interact—to shake hands or hug and say "Peace be with you"—I don't recall any laughter or expressions of joy. . . . I indirectly inferred the norms governing my conduct, including my emotional displays.

Here, we witness the limitations around what can and cannot be expressed within this congregational context. We also perceive how these norms are not necessarily stated; they are inferred from the behavior of those around us. This does not mean explicit regulation does not occur—children, who are often the targets of emotional normalization, get the brunt of this. Hushes, looks, and reprimands come both from parents and other members of the congregation. This chastening has the effect of reinforcing emotional norms not only for children but for the entire community.

Upon entering the pulpit, the religious leader is often highly aware of the congregation's emotional norms. They not only observe and accommodate those norms but are also expected to enforce them. "Pastor, can you tell Ron to take Susie out of the sanctuary when she starts crying?" "Rabbi, I don't like all the enthusiastic clapping. It disrupts the feeling of worship for me." "Reverend, that last song was a dirge. I don't like feeling sad when I come to worship." There are many instances in which the leader is expected to model and impose the emotional norms of the community. Depending on the clergyperson's longevity and credibility in the congregation, they may be the figurehead for the emotional tenor of the space. They may be required to stabilize the emotional atmosphere, especially if, or when, it is disrupted—for instance, after an aggrieved person disturbs the worship experience. After the disruption ends, attention turns to the clergyperson to reestablish the emotional atmosphere and safety of the worship space.

For many religious leaders, the emotional norms in the congregation are intuitive, which is to say they only sometimes arrive at conscious awareness. An example here is my friend Alex, an activist and pastor with the United Church of Christ. I first met her at a rally protesting a sanction targeting LGBTQ+ people. When she first stepped onto the dais to offer her speech, her words came slowly and clearly. She spoke of the effects these sanctions would have on her own life as well as on the lives of those she cares about. As she continued to speak, I noticed her body began to move more freely. The pace of her language increased. By the end of the speech, she was fully animated. Her words were passionate, magnetic. The crowd hung on her every sentence. She left the platform to enthusiastic applause.

About six months later, I attended one of her services. The building was lit with sunlight behind beautiful stained-glass windows. The walls were painted white. Large banners with images of grapes, grain, and vines flanked the pulpit. The congregation members lingered in the foyer before taking their seats, warmly welcoming me to their sanctuary. I was eager to hear my friend preach, and it was not long before she climbed into the pulpit and shuffled some papers. She then proceeded to deliver a carefully researched discussion of a Biblical passage. Her tone was solemn, and her voice and pace had little variation. She did not move. The interpretation was solid and thoughtful, but it clearly lacked the passion she expressed at the rally.

I waited around after the coffee hour. Alex and I planned to get lunch, but we settled on a late breakfast. Over eggs and biscuits, I mentioned I noticed a difference between her speech at the rally and her sermon. I asked if she ever spoke with that kind of passion to her congregation. Her response was telling. She said, "You know, I never thought about it before. But no, it's just not that kind of place. They wouldn't know what to do with that." Her insight seemed to arise less out of considered conviction and more out of intuition. It was a felt sense of propriety or decorum, an embodied understanding of the shape of the emotional norms in her congregation. And it may have been the correct one—again, clergy are often attuned to the congregation's emotional norms.

Of course, just because these norms are intuited does not mean they cannot be brought into conscious awareness. If you are a congregational leader, you might try thinking about what emotional expressions would make its members uncomfortable. How would they receive a hot and fiery sermon about social justice? What about a grief-laden, lamenting sermon about a loss in the community? If you are a preacher, what if you started to wave your arms while you're angry? What if you raised your voice? What if a tear ran down your cheek over the expression of a loss? What if you wept openly? If some of these make you recoil or cringe, that is a good indication that you have touched the live wire of emotional norms. They are neither good nor bad; they just are. And they govern congregational culture.

Emotional norms are embedded in long-standing histories of interaction and behavior. I was especially keen to learn that anxiety over emotion in preaching extends deeply within certain segments of progressive religious history. Researching early Unitarian patterns in preaching led me to some fascinating findings. Here I will list a few instances of emotional regulation in this history as a case study. This sample is limited both in terms of social location as well as religious tradition, but it gives a flavor to some of the anxieties around emotional norms in certain early progressive pulpits. (An added benefit is that the language is quite lively and entertaining.)

- In an 1830 lecture, New England minister Ezra Ripley critiqued the tendency in progressive congregational sermons to be "generally long, & delivered in a dull monotonous manner, that attracted the attention of only the very pious & good." He insisted that it matters not "how much learning a sermon contains" but rather that it should "make people *feel* their moral obligations" (my emphasis).

- In an 1836 lecture, Rev. James Walker agreed, though he warned against "interlard exclamatory interjections with high wrought phraseology, as if the speaker were determined at all events to be excited or to appear so." As he put it, "Sympathy should be excited, but it should be done through the understanding."
- In an 1844 lecture, minister Charles Robinson gave one of my favorite critiques of progressive congregational preaching: Such "preaching is said to be cold and lifeless, wanting in interest and efficacy, wanting in power over the affections, wanting in those solemn and fervid appeals, which touch the heart, awaken the conscience, rouse all the religious sensibilities of our nature." But rather than chastise his colleagues, Robinson found these worries misplaced and set out to defend the sermon. Reacting to the lingering fervor of the Great Awakening, he insisted progressive Christians "should not work themselves up at all." Such overwrought emotion, he felt, lacked authenticity. He concluded that it is acceptable if clergy provide "wholesome but unstimulating food" to their congregations.

Whether these ministers reject or defend emotional norms, their statements show the long shelf life such norms have in certain progressive pulpits. Many congregations—whatever the faith and geography—still contend with expectations of emotional restraint nearly two centuries later.

It is tempting to view these emotional norms as politically neutral. But emotional norms extend beyond the unique habits and expressions of particular faiths—their implication within broader social structures surfaces concerns about power. For instance, philosopher Alison Jaggar's 1989 essay "Love and Knowledge: Emotions in Feminist Epistemology" argues that emotional norms regulate racial, gender, and class differences. Specifically, groups associated with overt emotional expression often find their social standing and credibility diminished. Jaggar writes, "Reason has been associated with members of dominant political, social, and cultural groups and emotion with members of subordinate groups." Emotional expression is considered less intellectual, civilized, and worthy of social recognition. Therefore, assumptions about emotionality are not neutral but rather reinforce prejudice and domination. Those deemed to have appropriate decorum and restraint are taken seriously, while others are not. Communities that are dedicated to values of equality and justice should consider this history when evaluating their own cultural norms.

The question of how one can challenge these norms—deeply embedded as they are in denominational histories and social structures—can make the preacher throw up their hands. Considering their pervasiveness, intimacy, and formal and casual enforcement, it is easy to feel dispirited by the prospect of changing norms. But doing so misses the ways that cultural evolution and change are always happening alongside the maintenance of norms. All cultural institutions, even the most seemingly intransigent, are in the process of being made. As philosopher and psychologist William James writes in *A Pluralistic Universe*, "What really exists is not things made but things in the making."

Here I will name a couple of different elements or tools that facilitate change. Application of each of these tools will be unique depending on context, but they are intended as helpful considerations for transforming emotional norms.

Folks may have an ambivalent relationship to the expectations of their cultural context. They may operate within the confines of norms while having conflicted or indifferent feelings toward them.

For instance, it is easy for me to name the subdued emotional atmosphere of the religious community I grew up in—both the congregation and worship leader rarely demonstrated a passionate emotional process. But every so often, this would change when the minister increased the emotional temperature around a social justice cause she cared about. I remember the first time she broke adherence to emotional norms. After a particularly difficult story, she paused for a moment to compose herself, and then her speech caught fire. She passionately stated her call to the community to care about the issue. Her heart was in it.

This act transgressed the emotional norms of the congregation. It could have easily been met with bafflement or pushback; sometimes people attempt to reestablish and stabilize norms after moments of challenge. But that was not the experience in my home congregation. Instead, people were captivated. Many leaned in. A tear rolled down the cheek of the person sitting next to me. And this highlights an important point: Ambivalent feelings accompany social norms. Seeing someone challenge said norms can be relieving, revitalizing, and even riveting. Habits congregation members did not even realize were restrictive are recognized as such. In these instances, the preacher may receive comments about how much the sermon resonated, and people may welcome the change. For some, it can feel like a sip of water in the desert.

Knowledge of and interaction with other cultures also create an opportunity for change. To understand the effects of such interaction, it may be helpful to consider a life unencumbered by cross-cultural influence. For instance, a fourteenth-century European peasant would likely grow up in a single town with a single church, in a single profession and a single home, with a single set of values, beliefs, and customs. It is possible that such a person would never encounter someone from another culture, faith, or way of living. The same cannot be said for people in the United States in the twenty-first century. Indeed, we live in one of the most pluralistic nations in the world, and in the era of globalization, cross-cultural interaction is a fact of life. What this means is people know their congregational context and culture, but they also know *other*. They know there are other ways to do things, to experience life and faith, and to express their emotions. Sometimes this leads to rigid understandings of who belongs and who does not—but not always, and not necessarily. In other cases, awareness of other ways of preaching and worshipping can permit a reimagining of one's own cultural norms. Instead of thinking, "This is simply how worship is done," people may know that worship can look and feel like many different things, which can lead to opportunities to experiment and try something new.

Norms sometimes change with conscious reflection, which requires first lifting the emotional norm out of intuitive enforcement and into conscious awareness. To do this, one must recognize that emotional norms are often maintained below the conscious level. For instance, it's rare to hear someone say, "That person violated the emotional norm of suppressing laughter in the service." Instead, one might hear, "That person is rude and inconsiderate of others." The latter comment is an irreflective reaction to the presence of emotional norms. One way of changing emotional norms, then, is to bring them to awareness and discuss them. One might ask curious questions such as, "Why do we interact in X way?" "When did you first learn that acting in Y way was how things are done?" "Who does it serve for our community to continue to act in Z way?" All of these questions bring irreflective emotional norms into conscious awareness. While it is important to recognize that reflection is not a panacea, reason should not be underestimated. Offering vocabulary and concepts to bolster reflection may give leaders and members important tools.

Cultural norms can also shift without conscious notice. Change happens all the time. One may think that a congregation has remained rigid in terms of its practices, that its worship feels the same as it always has. But especially in traditions that do not have a set liturgy, this may not be the case. Recently, I went back and read bulletins from thirty years ago, and I discovered previous ministers called certain elements different names, ordered the elements differently, and announced annual church events that have long since ended. I saw hymn titles I have never heard sung. All of this has changed without comment. It was a slow process of evolution—and this process can be used with intention. A mentor in ministry once said to me, “Do you know how to move the piano from one side of the sanctuary to the other without causing a controversy? One inch every Sunday.” While that statement can represent a stealthy if not manipulative impulse, it can also exemplify pastoral intention. Slowly introducing greater change can offer continuity while familiarizing incremental differences.

The good news is that passionate delivery is not an all-or-nothing affair. When I first changed my preaching style, I only incorporated brief intervals of passionate expression. As we will explore in the practical portion of this book, a brief, deliberate spike in emotional tone can be more effective than extended movements at a high emotional pitch, which also gives the preacher more capacity to cautiously shift emotional norms. Rather than fueling the impression that the preacher expects the congregation to become a different community with different norms overnight, continuity provides the bridge that allows congregants to follow along. Eventually, with patience, the piano reaches the other side of the sanctuary.

The Preacher’s Identity

Emotional norms also function differently depending on identity. Not every preacher is allowed the same range of emotional expression in every context. Tacit norms regarding gender, race, and sexuality shape which emotions are permitted and how they are expressed in the pulpit. Passionate preaching by an LGBTQ+ person will be received differently than a cisgender, heterosexual clergyperson. A Black preacher will be received differently than a white preacher. Preachers of various genders will be received differently from one another. Here I will explore some of the ways that gender, race, and sexuality facilitate and complicate emotional expression in the pulpit. By relying heavily on existing literature on preaching and identity, as well as conversations with others, I hope to center other voices when speaking of identities that are not my own. My intention here is not to speak for others, nor is it to exhaust every possibility for understanding these dynamics. Rather, I hope to enable a deeper appreciation of the burdens, resilience, and guts it takes to navigate this terrain, as well as to show a variety of approaches to passion and emotion in the pulpit.

As I mentioned earlier, grappling with my own religious history and identity motivated this book. I begin here not because I wish to center my experience but because I don't believe in discussing others' identities and vulnerabilities when I refuse to do so myself. And for me, sexuality played a major role in seeking greater emotional depth in the pulpit.

I came out the same year Matthew Shepard was murdered. Seeing the images of his body hanging on that Wyoming fence post incited fear that collapsed my shoulders, making me aware of the danger of speaking my truth. When I climbed in the pulpit for the first time—which happened to be the same year of the murder—I swallowed the razor-sharp advice to preach on anything but queer issues. The LGBTQ+ ministers I looked up to and respected most confirmed that this was the wisest course of action. In other words, talking about queer life, emotions, and experiences meant being pigeonholed. Even in Unitarian Universalism, which is an open and affirming faith, many felt restraint was the best option. The fact that my family and congregation were emotionally buttoned-up and generally didn't expect emotional flourish didn't help anything.

It took many years for me to fully come out and thaw out. It took marrying my first husband and becoming a widower at twenty-five. It took making community with friends who were kicked out of their homes, lost their jobs, died by suicide, and lived with and died from HIV/AIDS. It took reckoning with grief and rage and survival guilt for the lives of lovers and friends who were cut down, ignored, and erased. Eventually, I found I was no longer comfortable being uncomfortable with my feelings about all of this. I had to break through the hard crust and name the pain and devastation and lament. I also had to identify and touch on the joy and pleasure that makes queer life not just worthwhile but desirable.

And what I found was that queer culture makes room for all of that. Many sophisticated queer expressions feel their way backward into deep wells of loneliness and exclusion and pain and find shimmers of joy and hope as they cruise for utopia. What's more, these emotions are not simply felt but are also rendered poignant by the creativity of queer leaders, performers, and artists who have always transformed such feelings into heartbreakingly beautiful, rapturous expressions and testimonies. Moreover, artistic representations, such as the AIDS Quilt, can facilitate transformative demands. It's true that for white gay men such as myself, a focus on feelings—bleak or bright—can turn insular and self-focused, functioning as a stealth cover for an unwillingness to grapple with areas of privilege and failure to care about the experiences of others. But—and this remains my wild hope—shared grief and joy can also open the self to wider solidarities and transformative desires.

Homiletics has been slow to recognize queer expressions. This is in part because of the conflicts that rage within many denominations about the status of queer people. Simply welcoming LGBTQ+ people into congregations can be controversial, never mind appreciating their insights into life and worship. Even traditions such as Unitarian Universalism, which have grown dramatically in terms of being inclusive and welcoming, have not fully appreciated the possibilities of queer preaching. The number of books and articles on this topic is quite low; my own 2023 contribution to *Queering Christian Worship*, "Under the Preacher's Robes: A Queer Embodied Homiletic" is one exception, in which I argue that queer cultural expressions have much to commend the preaching art. What if preaching spoke with the force of weeping and rage at the graveside of someone who died from violence or medical inattention? What if preaching poured itself into the joy and resilience of Pride? What if preaching leaned into the transgression of queer performance art and ACT UP protests? The incomprehensibility of appreciating those expressions in many religious contexts speaks to the distance that has yet to be traversed.

Queer expressions in non-queer spaces are troubled. LGBTQ+ people are told from a young age that their very existence is wrong and that they need to alter the way they inhabit the world. The creation of queer-friendly spaces can feel like a breath of fresh air. It's hard to breathe that same oxygen in religious communities, especially ones that have traditionally excluded us. And so, a queer clergy member may choose to navigate non-queer religious spaces with different approaches. I feel relatively fortunate that my congregation welcomes discussion of and appreciation for queer culture, but other colleagues segment their lives and go fully or halfway in the closet. Frequently, the choice to do one or the other—to be in or out—relates to the subtle interpersonal cues received from a particular congregation. Simply because the sanctuary has rainbow stickers and banners does not mean it is ready to embrace queer culture as well as its emotions and passions. And this is often orders of magnitude more complex for trans people, genderqueer, nonbinary, and queer people of color. Nonetheless, queer culture offers a spectrum of options for preachers who choose to wade into the complexities and challenges.

Womanist and feminist homiletics scholars offer more fodder for thinking through embodiment, emotion, and preaching. Early works in this field emerged during the 1980s as women gained increasing visibility in the pulpit. These books were attempts to think through embodiment in relation to a discipline that favored masculine traits, styles, and expressions. Many of these writers were operating (and some continue to operate) within a gender binary. Unless otherwise noted, authors generally use *men* and *women* to mean cisgender men and women, a framework that is being opened by new insights into sex and gender, as well as the experience of preachers with trans and nonbinary identities. At the same time, I believe lifting some of these voices in womanism, feminism, and preaching can reveal greater possibilities for thinking through embodiment and expression and appreciating the courage of those who broke the mold.

Rev. Dr. Christine Smith, a pioneer in feminist homiletics, champions emotions that have been culturally coded as feminine and invites women to lean into those feelings. As Smith puts it, feelings of "vulnerability and care" have been suppressed in favor of masculine expressions and oratorial styles. Some early twentieth-century texts on preaching endorse traditional images of masculinity as a model for excellent preaching. In *Lectures to My Students*, Charles Spurgeon, a towering figure in the history of preaching, suggests avoiding "the method of enunciation said to be very lady-like [or] delicate." Such prejudice has limited women in the pulpit and elsewhere. Undoing this suppression, Smith writes, "is not a matter of luxury, nor merely an academic or scholarly venture; it is a matter of survival of the self for most women." Hers is a clarion call to expand emotional options and delivery styles for the sake of women in the pulpit. No doubt, some heed Smith's call and lean into a "different voice," embracing emotional forms that have been gendered as feminine.

Others suggest that such an understanding of emotion and gender requires greater nuance. Professor Leonora Tubbs Tisdale wrote on the ways that women have transformed preaching over the last half century. In her book *How Women Transform Preaching*, one of her interviewees, Sister Joan Delaplane, says, "What is significantly unique in women's preaching? I really don't have an answer except to say that the stereotypes . . . don't fit. To say that women's preaching is going to be more compassionate, more personal, more sensitive, I haven't found that necessarily." She goes on to say that while discussions of certain embodied experiences and metaphors tend to be unique, many traditional associations do not hold. This is especially true for emotional expressions. Her words give greater space for women and all people who do not find their emotional expressions anchored in narrow gender expectations.

Cheryl Sanders, a womanist ethics professor at the Howard University School of Divinity, argues a different perspective. In her research on Black preaching, she discovered evidence for different preaching styles among men and women. In her view, men tend to focus on prophetic critique, while women emphasize storytelling and testimony. But this limited emotional range allotted by gender can be challenged in both directions. In "Preaching with Passion" she writes, "I concluded that men and women have something to teach and to learn from each other with respect to passion in preaching. Women's sermons can teach men to temper social criticism with compassion." She goes on to say: "At the same time, women can learn from men how to sharpen their own testimonies . . . with the cutting edge of prophetic indignation." While, again, we might wish to complicate a dualistic gender binary, Sanders's invitation is helpful. Her enticement to lean into prophetic indignation and critique can be an act of challenge, chipping away at the idea that righteous anger is off-limits because of gender. Cultivating an ability to express gentleness, compassion, and heart can further unravel toxic constraints.

Gendered societal norms inevitably shape conceptions of what is possible and appropriate in terms of emotional expression, and such norms cut in different directions. For instance, misogyny incentivizes men to deny emotions that are deemed feminine. As a result, some men refrain from expressing sadness even in cases of extreme loss. One cisgender male preacher I spoke with told me, "Even expressing too much happiness about things, such as a new baby in the congregation, can go against gender codes." Often, this self-policing is done because of how genuine emotional expression is received by peers. The expectation is that men will regulate their own emotions to maintain a masculine veneer—which does not hinder expressions of the anger or outrage commonly associated with passionate preaching. Overall, when it comes to preaching, men have more cultural scripts and supports to fall back on when compared with women, genderqueer, and nonbinary preachers. However, men embracing a broader circuit of emotions can entail its own risk, challenge, and courage. Modeling such expressiveness can be transformative and healing for congregants who feel shut up and trapped in.

As with gender, race encodes expectations about emotional expression. Since the 1970s, a significant body of literature has emerged about Black worship and preaching. These forms are generally more expressive than the moderation of white mainline preaching. The content and structure of the sermons lend themselves to greater emotional articulation in the pulpit; likewise, the community is often more willing to demonstrate the emotions that underlie the content. My own thinking about preaching draws from Black homiletic theorists who point out the limitations and even destructiveness of white mainline and progressive emotional norms.

Henry Mitchell shows in *Celebration & Experience in Preaching* that when a person hears a joyful song, they naturally wish to express the emotion. When their culture forbids their movement and vocalization, it severs the connection between the body and the emotional expression, between heart and mind. This is a kind of quiet violence, wherein participants become progressively disembodied and detached. It is, he writes, "a cultural inhibition to be pitied and a joy tragically squandered." Mitchell argues that people from all backgrounds can benefit from greater emotional connection and expressiveness.

Some clergy of color have entered predominantly white denominations and written about their experiences navigating the terrain. For some, this includes the culture shock of worshipping in an emotionally restrained context. One important book chronicling the experiences of people of color in a predominantly white denomination is *Centering: Navigating Race, Authenticity, and Power in Ministry*, in which author Rev. Darrick Jackson contributes his reflections on ministry and worship while exploring his journey into Unitarian Universalism. For Jackson, the mental focus of Unitarian Universalist preaching was jarring. "In the Black church," Jackson writes, "I experienced worship that engages body, mind, heart, and soul. But I see many [Unitarian Universalists] hesitant to engage the heart, the body, and the soul. They only want to stimulate the mind. They look for sermons that make them think and find sermons that stir the heart lacking."

Rev. Lilia Cuervo concurs in her own contribution to the book: "I now regret having suppressed for so long my passion and spontaneity in the pulpit, to the point that I doubt I can ever fully regain it." These clergy name the struggle to claim and reclaim embodied and expressive forms. As Jackson puts it, such attempts feel "risky and experimental" rather than worshipful. At the same time, Jackson's use of playfulness and improv theater in sermon crafting and

Cuervo's prophetic steadiness and determination represent pulpit creativity and vibrance in their own right.

People make a way out of no way. Lenny Duncan is a pastor with the Evangelical Lutheran Church of America and the author of *Dear Church: A Love Letter from a Black Preacher to the Whitest Denomination in the US*. In it, he gives a plea for greater passion about the subjects that matter and argues that insularity and apathy are killing the church. A large part of his work is dedicated to challenging his white colleagues who have fallen asleep at the wheel. Their lassitude aids and abets irrelevance and decline. At the same time, he speaks to his own lament and outrage and his willingness to put his heart and guts on the line while preaching. Indeed, his sermons are threaded with power and force. He advises his white colleagues "to preach as if our lives depend on it. My life absolutely does depend on it. . . . I know you can't preach a challenging revolutionary sermon every week, but that doesn't mean you never should." This advice speaks to the urgency and difference passionate preaching can make. A lot can hang on it. For Duncan, passion in the pulpit is both life-giving and lifesaving.

All of this is a mere opening to the conversation about preaching with passion and its relationship to sexuality, gender, and race. It leaves out many important identities and contexts and considerations. It doesn't address Dr. Kimberlé Crenshaw's notion of intersectionality, or any of the other important dialogues that need to happen. It presumes to offer no model for marginalized preachers; people must navigate these complexities with their own wisdom, resources, courage, and congregations. But I hope to center some of the ways preachers have created space for themselves as well as the diversity of what constitutes passionate expression, which can mean many things, take many forms, and entail many emotions. As womanist homiletics scholar Lisa Thompson puts it in *Ingenuity*, there are many ways "to attend to the totality of our beings in their cognitive, emotional, physical, and spiritual dimensions." That nuance makes for a richer portrait—one that would be missed if we were to breeze past the experience of preachers on the margins. And it lends new appreciation, I think, for the creativity and courage it takes to speak truth from the guts.

Authenticity and the Preaching Voice

There is yet a further hurdle many preachers must surmount, which has to do with one's self-understanding as a preacher. This issue is often framed as a question of authenticity. The conversation about what is and is not genuine, sincere, or true to the preacher's style and voice can influence which emotions are expressed in the pulpit. It is often live for preachers who do not view passionate expression as a typical pattern of speech and presentation. When I teach preaching with passion, I often confront a familiar concern: Many say, "I'm just not that kind of preacher." The worry here is that passionate preaching is not sincere or authentic expression—it does not fit with one's self-understanding, nor does it accord with others' expectations for that preacher. These routine concerns surface questions that are helpful to ponder. What is authenticity, and how does it relate to preaching? How does it intersect with emotional norms? And are there ways to think about authenticity that open possibilities for self-definition and change?

The first thing to note here is that the concept of authenticity is unstable. While frequently deployed, there is little consensus about its precise meaning. The concept came into widespread usage in Europe during the seventeenth and eighteenth centuries, which is when people first started to worry about being true to oneself—the result of a society that increasingly understood itself as an aggregate of individuals rather than an organic whole. Those worries immediately turned up contradictions and complexities evident in popular as well as philosophical conversations around authenticity.

While people often use the term *authenticity* as though its meaning is settled and self-evident, philosopher Alessandro Ferrara's 2002 book *Reflective Authenticity* has shown its unsteadiness. As we shall see, authenticity is less a self-evident fact than a collection of interchangeable meanings. Depending on which one the speaker intends, there is more or less room for self-expression and revision.

This is good news for preachers: Appreciating that authenticity entails complexities and contradictions can offer room in which to navigate. A more fluid understanding of the concept challenges notions of an authentic voice that is stable, self-evident, and linked to an unchangeable part of the preacher's self.

The conversation in homiletics about authenticity often relies on the notion of stable traits shown over time. Author Robert Stephen Reid captures this view in *The Four Voices of Preaching*: "Most parishioners come to see the pastor's passions, convictions, interests, questions, sensibilities, and affirmations as familiar perspectives that reflect the pastor's identity as a person of faith." Congregants learn of someone's authentic self because they have witnessed it on multiple occasions. They then create a narrative about what sorts of virtues and foibles the preacher will express, what sorts of interests they have, and what sorts of theological conclusions they will draw. The community further understands what emotions the preacher will show and how passionate the preacher will be.

Such a view helps to make sense of comments preachers receive. Congregation members may offer observations about traits they view as core parts of the preacher's demeanor, which may come as praise and affirmation: "She has such a comforting presence in the pulpit. Her voice is so soothing." Or they can be packaged as negative feedback: "His sermons are so plodding. He has such low energy!" Whether positive or negative, such qualities are fixed from the perspective of these congregation members. These traits comprise the preaching thumbprint that makes the preacher's approach distinct, recognizable, and consistent. Congregants would experience confusion or surprise if the preacher broke with these expectations.

But the notion of authenticity as consistent traits expressed over time is not without its own internal difficulties. Elements are stable within an identity until, well, they aren't. Some philosophers have leveled critiques against the idea of authenticity, arguing that emphasis on consistency and stability can ignore the self's evolutions and revolutions. These transformations are no less authentic to the preacher than the qualities that endure. This should be no spectacular claim; it is a truism that human beings grow and change. Indeed, many qualities in a preacher are not only changeable but desirably so—the point of studying preaching is presumably to change one's abilities for the better. Sometimes the changes suggested are trivial; at times they are dramatic. If authenticity were simply a matter of accepting the total cohesive package of who a person is, then these things could not be changed. But as a person learns, matures, and gains perspective, they might shift traits both consciously and unconsciously. The transformation of the individual may lead to greater awareness and expression of one's voice. In this case, change is the vehicle for greater authenticity, not less.

Worries over authenticity tend to spike when the clergyperson shifts their emotional expression. While changes in intellectual belief and theology can cause disequilibrium, they are often received differently from transformations in emotional presentation. Emotions are more often perceived as raw, primal, and impervious to intentional intervention. They cut to the heart, as evidenced in the different responses the preacher may receive. If, for instance, the preacher changes positions on an ethical issue, the congregation might ask, "What changed your mind?" If a preacher expresses lament for the first time and grief surges in the preacher's voice, the congregation would be less likely to ask this question—instead, members might engage in speculation about the preacher's psychology or major life changes. People imagine emotions to touch a core self, while thoughts seem less immediate.

In his 2014 book *Exorcising Preaching,* Rev. Nathan C. Walker worries over the expression of emotion and its relation to "being real" in the pulpit. He writes, "Preachers can become possessed. We approach the pulpit, open the text, and then suddenly our speech becomes exaggerated and breathy. The people in the pew cannot help but tilt their head and say to themselves, 'The preacher is really feeling it today.' " Walker interprets his pulpit experience as being "not only off-putting and annoying," but also "a barrier that prevents worshippers from making meaning." He calls for an exorcism of such inauthentic voices, which he dubs "the spirits of dead community theater actors." As he writes, "I was determined to be real when I approached the pulpit." In other words, Walker believes preaching is better done in the conversational voice—not necessarily emotionless, though its expression of feeling is toned down. Being real for Walker means defending against the perception that one is being overdramatic or performative.

Part of his concern may relate to the rhetorical notion of proportionality, the idea that not only the appropriate emotion but also the appropriate size of the emotion should attend our reactions. We might think about Aristotle's discussion of anger in the *Nicomachean Ethics*: "If we feel anger intensely or weakly, we are in a bad condition." For the philosopher, a skillful person expresses the right amount, at the right time, toward the right object. Too much, and the person is dismissed as raving. Too little, and it may seem the person lacks self-respect or compassion for another's plight. Here, the presentation needs to align with circumstance and display the right proportion. There is a joke about the preacher who, upon noticing the manuscript has started to bore, writes *pound pulpit here* to awaken people's attention, which would be a disproportionate use of emotion. Rather than aligning expression with a crest of emotion in the sermon's content, one distracts from sagging content with exaggerated gestures and expressions.

There are other anxieties that underpin this conversation and pertain to performance, its place in preaching, and its relation to authenticity. For some, performance and preaching ought not to be mentioned in the same breath. If the preacher rehearses or polishes their presentation—including their emotional presentation—they risk embodying, in the words of Walker, "dead community theater actors." They are no longer being real. This prejudice against performance is a live one among preachers and preaching theorists; Professor John S. McClure's edited volume *Best Advice for Preaching* features several theorists who rehearse these points. But this stance is controversial, and some homiletic scholars defend performative polish in sermon crafting, arguing that the preacher's performance deserves as much refinement as content and refusing to abandon preaching to a person's natural energies and mannerisms. Such a sentiment is akin to thinking a musician should refuse rehearsal because the rough edges make the performance genuine. Taken to its extreme, we arrive at the unfortunate notion that value and sincerity equate to lack of refinement.

The worry about performance in preaching revolves around the intentional crafting of expression such that it manipulates the sermon's receivers. As Professor Marguerite Shuster writes in "Truth and Truthfulness," "The sticking point with performance would seem to be the way the term brings to the fore connotations of self-conscious intentionality and artifice and perhaps emotional manipulation of hearers that mere talk of delivery may conceal." We thus arrive at something like the photo negative of authenticity, where performance seems to be the intentional evocation of something that was not there in the first place.

This discussion brings us to another concept of authenticity—the idea that what is authentic relates to a true self. Authenticity here is defined as the expression of a kernel that should be free from social interference, a kernel that is buried or obscured when someone seeks to manipulate perceptions through performative strategies. Performance entangles the self in interpersonal social negotiations that diminish a person's ability to be true to themselves. This is a familiar sentiment in homiletics—that authentic preaching expresses what is true to the self in a way that is plain and unadorned. Some say the preacher ought to just stand up and talk to people honestly about what they believe. Being real and expressing one's true self can represent an idea that effort equates with distortion. As Shuster writes, in these conversations, it is "as if whatever is done carefully or whatever is lovely thereby establishes itself as false."

This view's popularity does not translate into its validity. Human beings communicate in skillful and unskillful, clear and murky ways. For instance, there are times when one must exert great energy to articulate what is true. A person may feel that a loved one routinely misunderstands them. Their therapist coaches them on how to craft communication that is true to their experience; they may not know exactly what it is they feel until they talk through it. Then the person may need to rehearse the situation several times and receive feedback on when and how to share their emotions, raise or lower their voice, and stay in one place or move around. They may need help producing and arranging the words so the message feels right. Authenticity, in this instance, requires the work of social negotiation and translation. The true self is not simply hiding inside, fully formed, waiting for the person to pull back the curtain and show it.

Feelings, too, must be cultivated and curated. When the preacher expresses lament, outrage, and joy in a public moment, they would do well to discover ways to express those feelings convincingly. They may rehearse facial cues, verbal tones, and physical comportment that communicate the emotion. They may play at the edge of tears, such that grief is communicable but not consuming. They may enact anger and rage while pulling back from shouting. At times, they may be so invested that they must retreat from the emotion, so that they do not lose the ability to communicate by being overwhelmed by feeling. Such performance requires intentional management of emotional expression. The better one can perform an emotion, the closer one gets to authentically expressing it. The question is not whether one is "being real" (i.e., authentically expressing oneself) or "really feeling it" (i.e., acting); rather, it is a question of whether one is effectively or ineffectively communicating one's emotional response. And to communicate one's felt response, the preacher must craft and perform it.

Some fear that preaching with performative effort will come off as slick. Authenticity crumbles when the performance appears produced, fabricated, or manufactured. Preachers may worry that they will sound like a glib televangelist or glossy megachurch preacher. Such a perception damages what Aristotle calls the ethos, or credibility, of the speaker, which surfaces a further distinction—what I call the difference between affectation and expansion. Affectation is the cultivation of a mannerism that would not emerge organically from the preacher's demeanor, no matter the context. For example, no matter how deeply I feel about an issue, I would in no case begin expressing myself with the manner and speech of an aristocrat from the show *Downton Abbey*, a surly circus ringleader, or a sprightly talk show host. While these presentations may or may not be genuine for others, they are certainly not genuine for me. There is no meaningful connection between my felt experience and the mannerism.

By contrast, expansion assumes that, under the right circumstances, the preacher's expression may change. If I am especially heated about an issue, I may express larger, more intense traits. My voice becomes louder, my posture upright, my gaze focused. I may choose to cultivate aspects of that expression to be more effective, even larger and more intense. All of that would be an expansion of the personality because it relates organically to a feeling state. Affectation, by contrast, is an expression in search of a feeling. It does not connect organically with a feeling state and can be read by others as awkward, false, or slick.

Sometimes preachers ask me how they will know when a feeling state requires expansion. When is the performance of a fuller passionate expression required if that is not routine for the preacher? My answer here is twofold. First, return to the chosen topic of the sermon. This question requires psychic introspection about one's felt response to the issue. For example, following the outbreak of war in Gaza in October 2023, with images of violence and bloodshed saturating the news, my emotional state included desperation and grief. To express myself authentically, I knew I had to find a way to embody those emotions, which involved expanding the emotional presentation of grief in the sermon and expressing lament that was relevant to the situation. For people who wonder whether a passionate response is appropriate, it is crucial to ponder one's emotions in response to the topic. In the instance of the Gaza sermon, we are talking about the destruction and endangerment of thousands of lives. If that does not draw forth a powerful felt response, one that convincingly expresses sadness, we might wonder what will. I would argue that a reserved, distant intellectual presentation may well be disproportionate in such a situation.

Second, consider aliveness as a viable metric. What makes you feel awake and alive in your body? What plucks the most exquisite chords of your lived experience? Abiding by assumptions about what is correct and appropriate can trap us inside unhelpful expectations; even the injunction to be real can be a cover for habits and expectations that no longer serve. Likewise, adopting an affected presentation is unlikely to make us feel more alive and connected to our emotional states.

Instead, I want to encourage preachers to experiment with voice, expression, emotions, habits, and performance until they find methods and models that make their hearts race. I hope people find the techniques that are especially effective for them, that touch the heart and tug emotions up and out. Some of these approaches will stick; some will not. That's all for the good. This is how we learn and grow as preachers and human beings. And that's the only way to approach authentic passionate expression if it feels foreign to the preacher at first.

3

I GOT A GUT FEELING ABOUT THIS: SOURCING THE PASSIONATE SERMON

When I first asked how to preach with passion many years ago, I assumed the answer would be in the delivery. After all, highly effective passionate preachers are remembered for the powerful and dynamic presentation of their words. If we were to listen to a recording of Prathia Hall's sermon "A Nightmare in Broad Daylight," we would witness the cadence, rhythm, and power expressed in the delivery. It might seem, then, that the necessary ingredient for an effective passionate sermon resides in the presentation.

To an extent, that assumption is true; we will spend much time on the dynamics of delivery. But when preachers carefully ponder what makes the delivery successful, they realize there is more to it. Emotive preaching also requires careful attention to structure, evocative language choices, and the inclusion of texts and stories that facilitate a passionate process. All of these have to align to create a successful result.

And so we start by pulling out our shovels and excavating the core of the passionate progressive sermon: the skillful interpretation of sacred texts and the empathic connection with the gathered community. Let's break ground.

Disruptive Readings: Interpreting Sacred Wisdom

Progressive religious leaders are a diverse company, so much so that one may argue the label is too broad to be meaningful. These preachers may belong to liberal, mainline, Catholic, and even Evangelical denominations. They may come from progressive Islam; Reform,

Reconstructionist, and Humanistic Judaism; Buddhist lineages; my own Unitarian Universalist tradition; and many others as well. The fold is necessarily expansive—no one faith stamps a trademark on progressive values. Preachers from a variety of communities argue for hospitality to immigrants, liberation from economic oppression, LGBTQ+ justice, and reproductive freedom; they compose sermons that are antiwar, anti-imperialist, antiracist, anti-assault weapons; they argue for environmental care and climate justice. Individual preachers may add or subtract issues from their focus, preach them in combination, articulate them differently, discuss them regularly or on occasion, and disagree with one another on content, approaches, means, and ends. These preachers may be on the same side of one public demonstration and opposing sides of another. As I stated earlier, I am uninterested in drawing boundaries around terms. Instead, I am interested in how preachers articulate values of hospitality, liberation, justice, and equality with passion and force.

Because of this diversity, progressives use a variety of resources to preach a good word. Many works on homiletics assume Christian scripture as the sermon's core inspiration. While my own examples draw heavily from Christian and Hebrew texts, I make no assumptions that passionate preaching is limited to them, in part because of my theological footing—Unitarian Universalist preaching exegetes broadly, drawing from many texts and spiritual sources—and also because of my experience. At an interfaith event, I heard powerful words from the local imam, who made a strong statement against environmental racism by drawing on the language of the Qur'an. I have heard Jewish leaders use the words of the prophet Isaiah to argue for justice for immigrants. I have heard a Buddhist leader make a compelling case for reproductive freedom. And I have heard preachers from my own tradition of Unitarian Universalism use its insights to argue for equal marriage and LGBTQ+ protections. Progressive faith and preaching draw deeply from diverse wells.

I resonate with Frank A. Thomas, whose 2018 book *How to Preach a Dangerous Sermon* advances a broad social ethic of preaching. He is attentive to his own tradition of Black preaching, which relies on Christian scripture. However, he recognizes a pluralistic age needs a generous understanding of homiletics and preaching, so he celebrates preachers from many traditions that use various sources of insight. Rather than one set of scripture, he speaks of "the wisdom of ancient texts, the sources of ancient wisdom and truth, the wisdom of the ages." Yet this expansiveness does not make such wisdom optional—without it, the sermon becomes less potent and some of its nourishment disappears. Preachers may end up sounding not quite like themselves, slipping into the register of the motivational speaker, politician, or philosophy professor. Sacred wisdom contained in religious texts offers the homily distinctness and potency.

However, textual interpretation can be a challenge for progressive preachers who must contend with entrenched readings. Much interpretation, as Lisa Thompson writes in *Ingenuity*, "recirculates polluted air that is connected to troublesome social histories and relationships that eventually lead to the demise and erasure of some persons and ultimately communities." This bad air that hangs over the text is surprisingly difficult to dispel in theological or secular contexts. It is present when, for instance, one takes refuge in the text's divine inspiration and traditional meanings to resist social change. Here one might inveigh against women's ordination from a reserve of traditional arguments. But it also happens in secular contexts. For example, a teacher including Biblical literature in the high school curriculum might rehearse anti-LGBTQ+ conclusions not because they are historically accurate but simply because they are well-known. Progressives who engage with the text will thus fight an uphill battle against interpretive frames that have stabilized over time and often align with structural injustices. Without critical tools, interpretations may slide back to affirming rather than challenging unjust social patterns.

Progressive preachers committed to the project of liberation and justice need sharper tools. We need techniques for dispelling the polluted air and inherited assumptions. In that spirit, I suggest an approach that values the text not for the ways it confirms inherited assumptions but for the ways it upsets them. The power of the text lies precisely in what it disorients, disrupts, and disconfirms—it appreciates that these words from another land, another time, and another context can speak unruly, troublesome utterances to us. They can, if we let them, upset accepted theological conclusions and unjust social arrangements. The progressive preacher can praise the text precisely for its capacity to reflect truths back to us in poignant and unsettling ways.

Despite established theological and cultural frames, there is something deeply alien about the sacred text. I think here of the words of Albert Schweitzer, a Biblical historian who wrote the following words about Jesus in *The Quest for the Historical Jesus*: "He comes to us as One unknown, without a name, as of old, by the lakeside, He came to those men [*sic*] who knew Him not." Schweitzer continues, "He will reveal himself in the toils, the conflicts, the sufferings which they shall pass through in His fellowship, and, as an ineffable mystery, they shall learn in their own experience Who He is."

It is important to note that Schweitzer was neither a mystic nor a pious traditionalist. Instead, he was one of the figureheads in the First Quest for the Historical Jesus and was versed in the methods of scholarship that tried to uncover and demystify the historical person of Jesus behind the doctrinal overlay. And yet, in using these words to end his lengthy tome, he acknowledges there is a mystery, an impenetrability that remains even after the last line is written in the history book. That fundamental strangeness—that capacity to unsettle and startle—contains a hope that the text can never be domesticated by restrictive agendas.

Appreciating the unfamiliarity of the text is especially rich territory for progressive preachers who often contend with entrenched conservative readings. They can use it to challenge inherited theological assumptions that marginalize and exclude, of which there are many examples from multiple traditions. Elisabeth Schüssler Fiorenza's 2007 book *The Power of the Word* shows the ways Jesus challenged the interlocking systems of Roman domination and empire. She argues that Jesus opposed hierarchy, violence, and gender oppression. Farid Esack's *Qur'an, Liberation, and Pluralism* demonstrates that passages in the Qur'an should be reinterpreted for purposes of pluralism and the struggle against economic and political domination. Marc Ellis's *Toward a Jewish Theology of Liberation* argues against the idolatry of affluence and power and finds evidence in the Hebrew Bible for solidarity with the poor and dispossessed. Each of these approaches destabilizes assumptions that the sacred text justifies social domination and violence or offers nothing relevant about politics and power.

It is no doubt true that the people from long ago did not live under current systems of white supremacy, Western colonialism, and global exploitative capitalism. Their circumstances and ours are worlds apart, which should end any illusion that we might find a tidy set of rules by which to live or a guidebook to deal with injustice. What Jesus or Buddha or Muhammad would do now is impossible to know. And yet, in their apartness, contemporary readers might discover glimmers of similarity to the present. This similarity and difference, sameness and otherness, cannot be separated without draining the reading of its power. Become too friendly with the text, too certain about what it means and says, and it loses its capacity to startle. Gone is its ability to reflect something new. Try to remove the sameness and turn it solely into "history"—into difference—and what seems nailed down in the past slides again and again into the present. If we attend to the ways the ancients struggled with life, faith, social hierarchy, and empire, readers may discover novel ways to navigate the trials of our time.

To appreciate the text as unsettling also means appreciating it as unsettled, resisting both doctrinal and historical certainties. Indeed, many historians reject certainties as an option for scholarship. Instead, they speak of wagers, possibilities, and potentials—claims that cannot be settled for all time. These thinkers recognize that every culture is shaped by historical assumptions that differ from other times and places. The idea that one can achieve neutrality in relation to the text ignores the process of enculturation that shapes human understanding. In William Herzog's *Parables as Subversive Speech,* he writes, "It seems increasingly obvious that the claim to objectivity is essentially a rhetorical ploy to assert the authority of an argument, and because all efforts to remain neutral actually serve the interests of some group, it is impossible to take refuge in neutrality." Readings that assume neutrality short-circuit rather than facilitate reflection on the conditions that allow them to emerge in the first place.

Part of this reading strategy means appreciating contradiction and instability within the text, attending to the ways that different passages dispute and undermine one another. For example, many Christian readers are fond of the passages where Jesus makes claims about being the bringer of peace. When he proclaims that one should turn the other cheek, that is sometimes understood as endorsing passive behavior. At the same time, Jesus makes striking and contradictory claims, such as when he says he arrives not to bring peace but the sword. One easy solution to this conundrum is to choose the passages that align with one's personal preference; we may read the lines about peace and ignore those that say something different. But another approach is to savor the difficulty. How do the passages that make us uncomfortable challenge inherited readings and cultural bromides? Have we been convinced, for instance, that Jesus always and only advocated for passivity? If so, who does that serve? What are we to make of the passages that read differently? Some scholars take these questions to heart, arguing that Jesus's message was much more adversarial and antagonistic than many readers notice. Richard A. Horsley's *Jesus and the Powers* asserts that the prophet was deeply concerned about empire and power, and his solutions to it were confrontational.

My point here is not to settle on a particular reading of this question. Instead, I wish to notice that by allowing the text to be unsettled and unsettling, to offer contradictions and disputes, we gain a fuller concept of the text's potential meanings.

Few readers of sacred texts, progressive or conservative, will readily sign on to the notion that their reading simply confirms their worldview, but it is still the case that certain reading approaches are more amenable to disruption than others. Some tilt more readily toward the iconoclastic, contradictory, and unruly. And there is reason to prefer these strategies: The choice to read the text for its instability emerges out of a conviction that doing so is freeing. Inherited frames that function to organize power and disadvantage the socially excluded and marginalized have the potential to crack and dissolve. Well-worn anti-Semitic readings of scripture, views that support the subjugation of women, and interpretations that endorse slavery have been widely discredited. Interpretations that enforce social hierarchy and prejudices have been destabilized with new approaches. Appreciation for instability and disruption can favor those who have been the victims of inherited meanings, ossified through liturgical and interpretive repetition.

The challenge for progressive preachers is to locate techniques that upset and startle. Too often, the interpretations one learned in Sunday school or religious education classes sit on the reader's nose like a pair of glasses, difficult to remove. Techniques and methods are needed that allow the preacher's views to be disrupted by the text.

One approach is to change the interpreter's identification within the text. It is easy to read scripture, or any work of literature, and identify with the righteous; this can be true for conservative readings that pit Christians against the sins of the modern world, but it can also be true for progressive readers. A relatively privileged reader may identify themselves with a poor and dispossessed person, such as those the prophet Isaiah defends. And yet when that person reflects on their entanglement in systems of oppression, including that of global capitalism, they might feel uncomfortable proximity to the very people Isaiah rails against. Suddenly, we aren't the heroes; we're the villains—and that can be more jarring and potentially transformative than a ready identification with the oppressed. If a reading fits too comfortably with one's ideological commitments, it is possible the reading has become too domesticated, too confirming. The One unknown has again become the One we all know.

Another practice is to rethink and specify categories mentioned in the text. Certain passages about, say, workers and children can reiterate problems of exclusion. A passage about workers may be interpreted to mean workers with national citizenship, excluding recent immigrants. Passages about children may be understood to exclude children with marginalized identities. Specifying who those groups include can dispel the ideological haze that hangs over the text.

I will offer an example from a recent sermon I preached following a week when multiple states began considering bans on gender-affirming care for children. My own congregation includes trans members and nonbinary children, and parents and allies were grieving the new political reality. My sermon rejected the "Save Our Children" narrative being advanced by some conservative voices.

That message, I argued, was being promoted at the expense of other children who were singled out and maligned. I began by reading Matthew 19:13-15, the passage where Jesus implores the children to come to him. I then closed the sermon by reframing the narrative:

> People were bringing little children to Jesus for him to place his hands on them, but the disciples rebuked them. This is because the governor had passed a law against assisting trans kids. When Jesus heard this, he was indignant. He said to them, "Let the trans children come to me, let the children scorned by discrimination and hate come to me and do not hinder them, for the kingdom of God belongs to such as these. Truly I tell you, anyone who will not receive the kingdom of God like a trans child will never enter it." And he took the children in his arms, placed his hands on them and blessed them.

This reframing opposes the way Christian texts have been leveraged to pass regressive laws and harm the trans community.

A further technique is to engage with texts that have problematic aspects—to choose the hard or unexpected text. In "A Hispanic Perspective," liberation theologian Justo L. González advises preachers not to "manipulate the selection of texts so as to preach only from those that are easy and obvious." Choosing the hard or unexpected text can mean picking texts that feature violence, exclusion, degradation, and harm. Honestly grappling with these texts can provide insight for understanding and transforming difficulty and pain. It can model nuanced ways not to take the text at face value and instead offer ways to reframe and rethink the passage. By showing complicated legacies and offering better interpretive options, progressive preachers can engage approaches that produce a more humane outcome. Often, this means reading the text against itself—looking for the moments that call one beyond bloodshed and heartbreak. At other times, such readings can rely on the legacy of interpretation and the various ways people have resisted violent conclusions.

Reading texts with folks from different social locations can also jar inherited understandings and certitudes. Some refer to this approach as the pluralism or democratization of reading. A part of the question here relates to authority—who has the authority to interpret? Previous ages might have answered that with ecclesial authority, while, more recently, scholarly authorities are also considered credible. But recent interpretive strategies open the frame. These approaches argue that delimiting credible interpreters is, like the claim to neutrality, an exercise in power. It excludes the voices of those whose interpretations may produce disruptive conclusions.

In "The Neglected Interpreters," Justo L. González and Catherine González write about the radical interpretations that emerge from communities reading scripture in Nicaragua, which have "an ability to see what scholarly commentators hardly ever note, which seems to prove the contention that the poor and the oppressed have an edge when it comes to understanding the meaning of the Bible." The article argues for an appreciation of readers who come from backgrounds that may be very different from the preacher's own. These readers, while perhaps lacking formal training and position, can offer startling conclusions about the text.

These techniques assume the preacher does not accede too early to scholarly interpretations, which sometimes foreclose rather than open potential meanings of the text. Scholars can trap a text in the past, turning its statements into fossils. In *The Word Militant*, Walter Brueggemann claims that after all is said that can be said about theological and historical points, the reader is left with an utterance. We might know everything there is to know about the life of Jesus and the history and geopolitics of ancient Rome and Palestine, and we are still left with this line from Luke 6:24-25 NIV: "But woe to you who are rich, for you have already received your comfort. Woe to you who are well fed now, for you will go hungry." So what are you, dear preacher, to make of it? How will you testify? Perhaps this statement threatens to break free from historical confines and convict us in the present. Perhaps the ruse of historical distance disappears, and one cannot help but feel called and called out by the utterance. Perhaps it threatens to exceed historical boundaries and theological explanations and offer a fresh word.

The idea of relying on multiple perspectives and rejecting certitudes can make some preachers and theologians squirm. The unsettledness of truth can be an uncomfortable thing to abide because it can seem that such readings turn truth into perspective. "Your truth is different from my truth, which is the same as saying that there is no truth"—certainly not a position I wish to advance. For many progressive preachers, myself included, this relativism cedes too much ground to the ideological and theological pilings of injustice. A theological position such as, "This person is poor because God despises them," is not simply a true statement among other true statements. Just because someone believes or feels that to be true does not make it so. Rather, it violates what I take to be the message—proclaimed through many religious traditions—that suffering and poverty are not sanctified. It is the habits and systems that degrade and oppress that stand condemned. The question becomes, on what ground can one make that claim?

In Anna Carter Florence's *Preaching as Testimony*, she writes that claims are always made against counterclaims. Determinative truth claims, the ones that sound as though they are universal and for all time, are always made against other possible assertions. As she says, "There is a dispute between two parties, or a struggle of opinion, although neither testimony can ever claim absolute certainty; only probability." Therefore, testimony for Florence is the notion that someone will wager one truth claim over another; their experience, knowledge, and faith compel them to do just that. We might notice the different texture here between this argument and the above. It is one thing to say, "What is truth?" and shrug, deciding that no such thing exists. It is another thing to say the totality of my life experience—my whole intellectual and emotional grasp of world and faith—compel me to make this particular claim. I am willing to testify to it. Preachers may be unable to achieve certainty beyond this kind of claim, which seems to be thoroughly established in a pluralistic age. But saying this does not mean that every claim achieves equal truth or worth. The preacher must risk the truth known in the guts and state it against opposing assertions.

Such a truth must take the shape of a conviction. A passionate sermon is fueled by conviction; it is not a whimsical exploration of options or an indifferent philosophical exercise. Rather, the preacher must winnow the spiritual wisdom of the text to a point of committed belief. It is this assertion, this truth known in the guts, this wager grounded in one's felt experience, that powers the passionate sermon. This does not mean that the passionate sermon is humorless or that it cannot be playful at times, but it does need to ring with conviction. I often encourage preachers to frame the sermon topic in terms of "I know this much to be true." What is the "this much"? It should be a stake in the ground, a sharp point that nails the sermon into a fundamental conviction. It is from that point that the preacher announces with clarity and authority their truth statement against other options—the point that pierces claims and habits that harm others and diminish life. It forms the sharp edge of the passionate sermon.

Stating one's conviction is another term for going out on a limb. Preachers are often called to say improbable things that violate convention and common sense, and the preacher's message can seem foolish when set against the received consensus. They take seriously the texts that proclaim jubilee and release from debts, judge the wealthy and indifferent, prophesy the end of empires and kings, prioritize the penniless and the resident alien, and call for a community that heralds equality. Preaching these convictions necessarily makes the preacher sound like a naïf. As Charles L. Campbell and Johan H. Cilliers put it in *Preaching Fools*, preachers are fools "whenever we stand up to preach with nothing but a word in the midst of a world shaped by armies and weapons of mass destruction." We are fools when we contend with experts who insist that faith convictions are simply not pragmatic or workable. We are fools when we give a word of hope amidst circumstances that seem doomed to everyone else. We are fools when we address big issues from small pulpits. The preacher's task is to testify surprising, unsettling, improbable truths anyway. It is to be always a little over the top and out of our depth. It is to state the conviction while accepting accusations of idealism, absurdity, and naïveté.

It's important to note that these convictions do not always neatly align with progressive causes. Reading for rupture provides an equal-opportunity punch in the gut. When this technique is well executed, the sermon disrupts political certainties of all kinds. We witnessed this already in the reading strategy that changed identification in the text. No longer is the progressive community on the side of the oppressed; instead, it finds itself uncomfortably on the side of the victimizer, upsetting any self-righteous assumptions. The benefit of such approaches is that no political paradigm or identification becomes too safe. Such reading strategies contest political agendas that have become sedimented, upending established theological interpretations as well as progressive slogans. The hope is that such approaches open new horizons for justice seeking that current efforts fail to notice. Done well, they should both deepen and challenge progressive theological and ethical commitments.

Empathy: Sourcing the Message

The great contemporary preacher Barbara Brown Taylor argues that there are three components of any sermon: the preacher, the people, and God or the sacred. "The stool of my sermon," she writes in "Preaching," "rests evenly on those three legs." Without any one of those elements, the sermon becomes lopsided and unstable and risks crashing down. If this is the case, then the preacher needs to find ways to bridge the gap with the sacred. In the previous section, I explored methods that assist the preacher in accomplishing that. By seeking messages that disrupt, the progressive preacher can find fresh ways to interpret and engage the sacred in the preaching moment. We are then left with the other leg of the stool: the people. How can the preacher locate a shared emotional connection that will be meaningful to those who arrive for worship?

What this means in practical terms is that sourcing the message is not solely an exegetical process. Nor is it a question of autobiographical exploration, theological critique, or intellectual creativity—elements that are important but secondary to a more primal reality, which is the empathetic connection the preacher has with the people. If the preacher fails in this effort, they will be adrift while reading sacred texts and searching for contemporary resources. The preacher must risk an empathetic understanding of the questions, hopes, pains, and joys of the congregation to offer a good word. In *Practicing the Preaching Life*, David B. Ward writes that without empathy, "The preacher may discuss a question no one is asking, solve a problem few are facing, or clarify an ambiguity no one is feeling." The preacher is, in other words, lost in the wilderness without a compass. Empathy allows the preacher to understand what emotional and theological concerns people will bring when they encounter the sermon; it is the needle that points the preacher in the direction the congregation needs to go.

A lack of empathy causes the sermon to run aground for two reasons. First, the preacher may miss the pastoral concerns of community members and thus fail to craft a relevant and sensitive word. Ward gives an example of this: In a bulletin, someone once published the sermon title, "All Things Work Together for Good." One look at that, and a man who had just lost his wife to cancer gathered up his children and left. While no preacher can understand every person's condition upon entering the sanctuary, empathic consideration turns the preacher again and again to the experience of the people. It breaks through hollow bromides and theological clichés to address the needs of the heartbroken. It lessens the possibility that the preacher will leave in the dust those most bruised and hurting.

Second, without empathy, the preacher may miss the needs of the broader social context and fail to bear witness to the pain and suffering in the world. When this happens, preaching detaches from urgent realities and fleshy concerns and floats away on ethereal currents—or it becomes an insular affair, losing itself in the cul-de-sac of the preacher's pet topics and congregational anxieties. To head off these eventualities, preaching efforts must be sourced from concerted empathetic engagement. The passionate sermon must cultivate openness to the experience of others in the congregation and the wider community.

The incorporation of empathy also pertains to the stories preachers use. Homiletic literature is full of techniques for reading sacred texts, and some spend considerable time on how the preacher should unpack ancient narratives. Understandably, these preachers treat sacred texts with respect and reverence. Sometimes, though, the same preachers give less care to stories from the present, manhandling anecdotes that support the message. Indeed, there are compendiums of "illustrations" that can be readily plopped down into sermons and often have the same quality and consistency of canned food: overly processed and wanting in nutrition. What's more, they can fail to be sensitive to the subjects of the stories.

For instance, in one sermon, I remember hearing a story about a person who had experienced intimate partner violence. The preacher concluded it with an ending that sounded like it came from a Hallmark card, skirting over the challenge and struggle of the person in question. Perhaps the preacher did not have access to those details—which suggests that the source was incomplete and thus not appropriate for the preaching task. A fulsome story offers a deeper and more complex understanding of another's experience, not a convenient fable. The sermon that incorporates this fullness will hold a more humane message.

Empathy is often understood as an imaginative projection into another's experience, relating to the connotations of its German root, *Einfühlung*, which translates literally as "feeling in." Originally an aesthetic notion, it had to do with the ability to "feel into" the emotional intention of an art piece. Eventually, this evolved into a moral consideration, the idea of witnessing someone else's loss or pain, for instance, and imagining how one might feel in that situation.

While this can be a helpful start for empathetic connection, it contains pitfalls. A generous response can be compromised when I assume my experience is universal. My own relationship to loss is different from that of another person. Therefore, empathetic connection requires curiosity about the lived experience of many others, which is an effort not anchored in projecting my interior experience. This requires that the preacher cultivate habits that turn again and again to the other: engaging stories, reading fiction and nonfiction, appreciating psychological insights, observing art, relishing poetry, and looking for the words of others that detail the fullness of human experience. Even then, emotional experience cannot be universalized. However, when the preacher seeks to empathize with the congregation to craft the sermon, a life of curious engagement will offer a fuller portrait and assist in the community's growth.

Skillful use of empathy requires a posture of humility. Too often, the idea of the preacher has been of the sage on the stage. This idea of preaching is a one-sided imparting of knowledge, where the preacher is the expert with all the answers. But this stance is surely flawed; no person is an expert on another's experience. Assuming otherwise can warp the agency and integrity of the people whose stories are included in the sermon. In these moments, preachers need approaches that help them get out of their own way. They need practices that subvert their role as the subject-presumed-to-know. This might mean inviting others to the pulpit to tell their own story, or perhaps it means the preacher sensitively includes other voices by quoting them with their permission. It can mean refraining from quick interpretations and skirting difficulties. This homiletic engagement should embody a posture of "I am learning as much as everyone else who is encountering this story; I am not the expert." While one can never fully comprehend and understand another's experience, empathy entails the continued striving to do it better.

Empathetic preaching cultivates awareness for the structures, habits, and speech that diminish another's personhood. This can be a challenging task for the progressive preacher because it often highlights gaps in one's own awareness. Receiving feedback that one has unwittingly used ableist, racist, sexist, or homophobic language can be disconcerting. A knee-jerk response might be, "I am a good person—I did not intend that." While the preacher may feel defensive and argumentative, empathetic preaching resists that impulse because such responses refocus attention from the issue (that the sermon in some way fell short) to the comfort of the preacher. While the preacher may reasonably desire such comfort, an empathetic sermon prioritizes a different goal: a language and practice that strives to embody the kingdom of love and justice. A better response to criticism is recognizing that any given sermon can miss the mark. Any particular sermon is imperfect. And the benefit of preaching consistently to a congregation is that the preacher, community, and their shared language, perspective, and experience always have the potential to grow in a more open and affirmative direction.

The practice of empathetic preaching trusts members both during and after the sermon. A sermon that respects and trusts does not assume agreement. Rather, the preacher is setting forth their truth as a wager. The preacher then has faith in folks to use their own experience and knowledge to accept or reject it, which means avoiding making both "you" and "we" statements in the sermon. Using "I" statements emboldens receivers to consider whether their heart and mind are in accord with the preacher. This stance prevents the preacher from colonizing the other's experience and assuming they can speak for all people. Such relational trust extends beyond the crafting of the sermon and is also part of the treatment of individuals after they receive the message. The preacher trusts folks to make of the sermon what they will. The time following the sermon is not for arguing details or rehashing debates; the preacher has said their piece, and they need to be at peace. Afterward, it is the member's turn to respond if they choose.

Empathy is trusting members to respond in their hearts, lives, and in community. This stance fosters an environment where the congregation knows they can safely disagree with the clergyperson and with each other. It also acts as a further guardrail against worries that passionate preaching will manipulate and bulldoze the integrity of the gathered community.

Preaching that empathizes with others requires courage. It is a brave thing to address the various experiences of those in the congregation—ones that may be hard to bear. Any given member may struggle with a range of issues that are not often discussed in public, including intimate partner violence, suicide and suicidal thoughts, depressive episodes, loved ones who died violently, addiction, drug use, PTSD, mass shootings, gang violence, abusive family, and prejudice. Likewise, members watch news stories and may come contemplating a range of issues, including climate crises, war, torture, sexual assault, famine, human trafficking, deaths of despair, genocide, drug cartels, humanitarian crises at the border, and bombings.

I am not mentioning these to be dramatic; these topics are borrowed from news stories I read last week. It is important to note that people are coming to congregations pondering the headlines. The preacher needs to exercise courage in addressing the various issues that arise, lest they give the impression that their faith has nothing relevant to offer.

Unfortunately, preachers can receive feedback that some folks "don't come here for that." Members may wish for less challenging sermons. The question then becomes: How does one address these issues in responsible ways? I have found that preachers have more success threading that needle when they respect and acknowledge that the topic is hard, voice that it is okay to struggle together and disagree on how to address the issue, and present opportunities to contribute to change. For example, the minister who preaches a sermon about intimate partner violence may mention that its statistical prevalence means that everyone likely knows a person affected. They may then point out the ways that keeping silent about such an issue contributes to more suffering, and hence it is important to break unspoken moratoriums. Finally, the preacher might then show members a way to contribute to and assist with the issue—such as highlighting local organizations—so that no one leaves feeling there is nothing to be done. While some might feel this is unnecessary padding on the sermon, I have found it essential to assist others in receiving the message; it is empathetic both to those directly affected by the issue as well as those finding out about it for the first time.

Sometimes, the issue that must be addressed will be both challenging and unavoidable. In 2022, five miles from my congregation, a person opened fire on a Fourth of July parade. Members of my congregation were in the parade and witnessed the massacre. It would have been unthinkable for me not to address it on Sunday. At the same time, I knew many people were traumatized; their sense of safety had been shattered. It was a painful week of pastoral care, as I spoke with dozens of congregants who were reeling. That Sunday, I realized an empathetic sermon needed to do two things. It had to admit to the heartbreak, and then it needed to embody a simple, straightforward message: "Never let the world beat the softness out of you." I focused on all of the vibrant, tender ways we are present, week in and week out, to care for each other, and I testified that no amount of violence could eradicate that. It was not the time for hard-hitting social analysis or theological pondering about evil. Instead, the moment required truthful reassurance and honesty about what was in my heart.

This conversation surfaces a preaching proverb that deserves reflection—the notion that the preacher should preach on scars and not on wounds. The sense here is that preachers ought to refrain from unprocessed, needy, messy expressions in the pulpit. To a degree, I appreciate the intention of the sentiment that the bleeding messenger distracts the congregation from the message. At the same time, I am not sure how preachers are expected to be both relevant and woundless. When horrors plague news cycles and the lives of congregation members, preachers may well need to preach on fresh pain. Sometimes, as with the Fourth of July shooting, there is no choice but to offer a timely word, even as the preacher's heart breaks. After all, someone who is wounded in a disaster may still assist others.

Two considerations can facilitate effective preaching in these moments. First, the preacher needs to ensure their own wounds are being treated; they need to seek support and help to process their pain. Second, the preacher can rely on their experience and strength to offer hope. They can preach on a truth that has pulled them through previous bleak moments. What, in previous moments of shattering, has proven unshatterable? Start there.

All of this can make empathetic preaching feel especially dramatic, even operatic. It can sound as though only the direst and loudest circumstances are worthy of the preaching moment. Indeed, that is a stereotype of passionate preaching—that its subject matter is larger than life and must be about grand issues, terrible crises, and dramatic happenings. But many things in the world provoke emotional connection, all of which can seed moving sermons. Paintings, nature, music, dreams, billboards, poems, theorems, embraces, newborns, textures, jokes, etymologies, conversations, injuries, and glimmers can all lure the preacher. And there is solid reason to notice and celebrate the everyday. In *Womanist Ethics and the Cultural Production of Evil*, Emilie Townes calls for the celebration of "the everydayness of laughter and joy" that challenges systems and habits that grind down life and drain away meaning. The empathetic sermon helps the congregation remember and experience those moments.

Whether the topic is grand or ordinary, the preacher needs to clarify why it is worthy of the preaching moment. Why does this group of people need to hear it? In many ways, empathy boils down to finding clarity about why *this* sermon is needed for *this* community in *this* moment. The seed of the sermon can fall on rocky soil when the preacher is unable to articulate in a sentence or two why it is relevant and timely. This step is crucial yet sometimes overlooked in sermon preparation. When the preacher fails to achieve this clarity, the homily can sound like a pleasant and interesting exercise, but one that is devoid of urgency. To head off this eventuality, the preacher can ask of their sermon: "Why this? Why now? Why these people?" Empathetic connection requires an understanding of the stakes (why this makes a difference) as well as the specifics (how it affects the community). Refining this element of the sermon prevents it from parsing an ambiguity that no one is feeling, answering a question no one is asking, and pondering abstractions miles away from the lives of those gathered. It sharpens and clarifies the empathetic connection, as well as the difference the sermon can make.

4

DO YOU FEEL ME? CRAFTING THE PASSIONATE SERMON

Some of my fondest memories of my grandmother include the times that she taught me how to bake. In her tiny apartment, we would pull out all the utensils—metal measuring spoons, glass bowls from a garage sale, and an ancient mixer that made an unholy sound when it started. We sat those next to the flour, sugar, milk, and butter, and then we would bake away. The results were not always met with parental approval: cherry pie, German chocolate cake, and the best chocolate chip cookies I ever tasted. With her careful eye, the treats usually turned out quite well. However, on one memorable occasion, I made an error. The recipe called for three tablespoons of butter. Without looking too carefully, I added three *cups*. The result was a blob, a sweet goo destined not for the table but for the trash. "We didn't get this right," my grandmother said with a laugh. "The structure is all wrong."

As for the baker, so for the preacher. Sermons can have an insightful start, they can interpret a text brilliantly, and they can be sourced from thoughtful empathetic connections, but they also need form. They need the appropriate language and structure so that the congregation feels what the preacher is saying. This chapter provides the necessary tools to craft the language and structure the sermon so the preacher does not aim for a sermon and end up with something else—something more like a sweet, formless goo.

The Language of Experience

Ralph Waldo Emerson's "Divinity School Address" is a classic text in preaching literature. He offered this speech to the graduating class of Harvard Divinity School as a warning to students not to live in the "sepulchers" of the past. He called on them to find language that pulses with life rather than rehearsing the thoughts and approaches of dead men. This tedious esteem for the past, he writes, blighted the sermons of too many ministers, including sermons that he personally heard. Emerson specifically states his distaste for one preacher, and his description is so severe that I find myself grateful not to have Emerson in my pews: "I once heard a preacher who sorely tempted me to say, I would go to church no more. . . . A snowstorm was falling around us. The snowstorm was real; the preacher merely spectral. . . . He had lived in vain. He had not one word intimating that he had laughed or wept, was married or in love, had been commended, or cheated, or chagrined."

Ouch. It's harsh judgment. So what exactly went wrong in the snowstorm? What tools could that preacher have used to save his sermon?

Elsewhere in the essay, Emerson defines preaching as "life passed through the fire of thought," a line that continues to resonate for many progressive preachers, suggesting that the preacher's own experiences need to be made vivid in the preaching moment. His ideas resonate with recent theories of preaching. Contemporary homiletics scholars such as Anna Carter Florence and David B. Ward prioritize what they call *testimony preaching*, as opposed to "memory sermons" that are preoccupied with what previous generations said and did. Memory sermons may spend time discussing the stories of saints and pioneers or pondering the theologies those generations handed down. Such sermons can become entangled in proving truths and arguing points, citing sources and quoting authorities. By contrast, the testimony sermon is grounded in the preacher's experience and prioritizes encounters with the holy as those show up in real life. Rather than rehearsing past deeds, pondering theologies, or restating doctrine, the preacher bears witness to the vitality of faith here and now.

This fundamentally changes what the preacher needs the language of the sermon to do. The language of memory can be rarefied and remote, while the language of witness needs to be vibrant and immediate. And indeed, Emerson's "Divinity School Address" uses language in just this way. He makes frequent use of a lyrical, even ecstatic prose. For instance, these are the first lines of the speech: "In this refulgent summer, it has been a luxury to draw the breath of life. The grass grows, the buds burst, the meadow is spotted with fire and gold in the tint of flowers. The air is full of birds, and sweet with the breath of the pine, the balm-of-Gilead, and the new hay." This is not the language of philosophy or theological doctrine—at least, not in the customary sense. It is not the language of intellectual disposition or propositional truth claim. Instead, it is the language of poetry or experience. It is lush. One is invited to feel the texture of hay and grass, hear the birds in the air, smell the summer pine, see the bursting buds.

By crafting an experience with words, the preacher can lure others toward the heart of truth, beauty, and goodness as it shows itself in our world, laying the groundwork for a sermon that witnesses the vibrant ways faith comes to life. Life passes through the fire of thought by passing into language. And this brings us to the next element in the process of developing a passionate sermon: the use of sensate language to craft the message.

The use of experiential language is more than crafting a few pretty but dispensable descriptions. Rather, it changes what the sermon is doing in fundamental ways. One way to think of the sermon is as an argument for theological concepts and propositions, which requires language that is simple, precise, and unadorned. But if the preacher does not primarily understand the sermon that way, then language can be made to do something else, like craft an experience or invite others on a journey. By sharing an experience drawn through vivid language, the preacher and congregation may arrive together at a new understanding. Perhaps the preacher and congregation reach new theological depths, but the sermon does not focus on clarifying abstractions. Rather, sensate language opens the way for a more holistic and emotional engagement. It causes the message to ignite in the minds and hearts of the gathered community.

As a corrective to the overemphasis on the rational in worship, some have issued calls for creativity and embodiment wherein the tactile and the sensate are accentuated in ritual elements and liturgical processes. This has been effective and can be put to great use. But I have also noticed that in some of these writings, preaching is de-emphasized and even devalued. Perhaps it is even made the foil of embodied ritual. Even philosopher James K. A. Smith, in his enormously thoughtful book *Desiring the Kingdom*, sometimes implies that preaching is separate from the embodied liturgy he promotes. It starts to sound as though liturgy happens at the ground level, in the body, aimed at the heart and gut, while preaching is a balloon that floats high above it all—the part of the service where everyone knows the head will be addressed with airy, bloodless abstractions. Liturgy engages the body and emotions; the sermon engages reason and ideas.

But a sermon that organizes itself with sensate, tactile language brings the balloon down to earth. Preaching is not the part of the service where the congregation departs to ethereal realms; it's where members fully integrate body, spirit, heart, and mind. By following Emerson's warning not to disappear into pale abstractions and spectral ideas, the sermon passes life into thought and then entwines the two. Preaching catches fire when it anchors itself in experience and enlivens that experience for the gathered community. It is not the antithesis of liturgy but rather its apotheosis, the place where worship becomes the grittiest, most alive, and most embodied because it activates all parts of the human being.

How does one achieve this effect with language? The experience of a body in the world of people and things is anchored in the five senses. While folks are differently abled, some combination of the senses creates what we call *embodied experience*. Someone hears, sees, touches, tastes, and/or smells an experience.

For instance, if the preacher is discussing a protest at an immigrant detention center, they could talk about the heavy crunch of military boots on the ground and the sight and sound of a camo-colored helicopter whirring over the chants of the protestors. They might smell the unsettling combination of car exhaust and honeysuckle outside the walls of the facility, taste the artificial sweetener of the electrolyte mix in a yellow-and-white bottle, or feel the indentations of the gray chain link fence pressed against their palms after being pushed by an officer in black leather-and-rubber riot gear. Using this kind of description is much more effective than the line, "I protested at the detention center." The former appears in the mind with life and color; the latter likely slips through the mind of the receiver like water through a storm drain. The challenge for the preacher is to create vivid language that captures experiences and catches in consciousness. Without this, the sermon may leave little trace.

Just as the use of tactile language creates the physical world described in the sermon, it also gives shape to interior states. Emotional experiences often evade description; there is a surprising lack of language to describe them. You might pause for a moment to think about how you would describe grief. You might describe where it shows up in your body and say it feels like a clench in the gut, or a compression of the throat, or a tension behind the eyes. But after you move beyond basic physicality, the only way to continue communication is through metaphor. The emotional experiences themselves are surprisingly devoid of shared understanding and language. Nonetheless, artful use of metaphor is a skill that can be cultivated. Novelists and poets are often adept at such interpretation and description. The preacher can make use of the same language, describing grief as swallowing razors, or a wave washing over and drowning the person, or being trapped behind a pane of glass apart from a loved one. When such description is used, the experience is released from its interiority and privacy and brought into shared language and space.

The incorporation of the senses in preaching can be done in a limiting way that discounts those without access especially to sight or hearing. When one sense is emphasized over all others, preaching runs the risk of insensitivity and exclusion. To avert this outcome, ask yourself if the sermon assumes that every person has access to the senses in the same way. If so, then the sermon needs to open and become more expansive. Kathy Black, who has written on disability and homiletics, challenges preachers to widen the use of the senses in preaching. For instance, in a communicative form that is highly attuned to the oral and aural, she encourages preachers to make use of the visual as well as other senses. For Black, "Preaching justice among people with disabilities also involves the language we use that can be either welcoming and accepting or alienating and judgmental." If the preacher keeps insisting that the congregation "open their ears to the message," it can be alienating to folks who do not have access to that sense. Referring to the sermon's receivers as "hearers" can be alienating as well. But if the preacher expands their language and metaphors and draws the message with words (and of course makes use of appropriate tools such as signing, visual aids, printed sermons, or captioning), that will open doors. By including multisensory descriptions while not assuming universal access, one can create a rich texture to their preaching that produces multiple entry points.

If vivid language is a powerful tool, it is also a tool of power. It can be wielded to create change. Walter Brueggemann, a prolific scholar of the Hebrew scriptures, used the Lyman Beecher Lectures on preaching to discuss language. In *Finally Comes the Poet*, he sets aside content, structure, history, and theology to discuss the choice and arrangement of words. He then shows that such choice has everything to do with history and theology. In one of his more provocative claims, he says the prophet could just as well have been called the poet; when the prophets spoke a daring word against monarchy or empire, they used the language of poetry to do so, rhapsodizing apocalypse, lyricizing destruction, and singing an end to despotism. They intoned the coming of a kingdom of fairness and justice, and it is through their language that people can feel the edges of it and imagine their way into something different. Brueggemann calls for the fashioning of language into a weapon against abusive power. The word pictures the poet creates become an "imaginative assault" on the indifference and cruelty of those who should know otherwise. Such speech ruptures the encrusted ideological and theological pieties that preserve political arrangements. They show the way to a new world. After power has been established and cemented into popular imagination, finally comes the poet to prophesy something other.

The ability to draw colorful images with words may sound trivial, something that belongs to dreamers. But its political relevance ought not to be underestimated. Sometimes the war over ideology is called a "war of ideas." Should health care be universal? Should marriage extend to same-sex couples? Should immigrants be given a path to citizenship? While these issues are called ideas in a broad sense, that label can be misleading, as though the battle happens at the level of policy. A more accurate thing to say is that the battle is happening at the level of imagination. The conversations on health care, marriage, and immigration pivot on the stories of people. When these situations are drawn with language in compassionate ways, people may extend empathy, but when these stories are drawn in vicious ways, the conversation shifts in bleak directions. It might be more accurate to label the war of ideas as a war over word pictures—who can draw them in the most compelling ways, and for what ends. And they are not only the politician's weapon; they are also in the preacher's arsenal.

So how does one create a word picture? In a recent sermon, I preached about the destruction of a ravine I had loved as a child. My aim was to set people up for attachment to this natural place so that lament for its loss and grief for other forms of environmental destruction would be possible later in the sermon. Here is its opening:

> Sprinting through yards and gardens, watching the sunlight spackled through trees on driveways and porches, turning cartwheels on the sidewalk until grit was embedded in palms, drawing elaborate chalk pictures and hopscotch grids, my friends and I run the streets of our neighborhood. Sometimes we depart from the checkerboard of lawns for the ravine. A hill dips downward until you find a creek at its bottom. We run/fall down the side of this rocky hill, getting scraped, licking the blood from a cut as its coppery taste blooms across the tongue. To traverse the water bed, we hop across stones; we take a vaulting leap. A rope lolls from the trees like a pale, white snake, one we grasp without fear as we swing our small bodies over the water. Sometimes we pretend our lands are divided by the roaring, gentle water of the creek. Sometimes we turn over the stones, the thick, pungent earth disgorging in the air, making the atmosphere smell of caves and buried things. The stones reveal the treacherous, fragile claws of crawdads. Nothing ruins our primal love for it all, this magnetic draw to be in and around the tiny part of nature suburbia abandoned to us.

A few things to notice here: First, the tense is present. Even though it happened over thirty years ago, I tell it as though I am back in it, running through the streets, which makes the picture immediate. Second, the movement engages the five senses. Maybe not all of them, but most of them. Third, there is action happening. Just because one creates a word picture does not mean that it must be still. Often, the more the scene "moves," the more one is drawn in.

A further consideration is about the time it takes for a word picture to become lodged within the receiver's mind. In David Buttrick's 1987 book *Homiletic*, he interrogates the conditions that allow for an image to catch in the consciousness and argues that the movement must have enough heft not to slip past notice. I liken this to an old-fashioned scale. As grains fall to one side, the weight increases, but only when the pile is large enough does the scale weigh enough to sink. An image weighs enough when time in the sermon is spent on it; only then does it sink into consciousness. You might notice the word picture above, the one with the details about the ravine, is about two hundred words, an appropriate amount of language for the image to settle into consciousness. It should be noted that this is true for other elements of a sermon as well, including the development of theological points and discussion of sacred texts. The spoken word requires more time to emerge and settle within the consciousness than does the written word. Brief quotations and quick references often slip past awareness.

Here are a few other tips that can be helpful when crafting descriptions so that they stick with people:

- **Do not pack all the senses and sensate descriptions into the first couple of lines.** Unfortunately, this often has the effect of making the exercise sound effortful, as if the preacher is trying to do something fancy with description, which kills the effect it otherwise might have. It is better to scatter the senses through the story, making the effort less noticeable.

- **Know how to use clichés.** While clichés are sometimes acceptable as a method to set a conversational tone, they are terrible when used to communicate anything of substance or meaning. They might be thought of as dead metaphors—figures of speech whose vitality has been drained from overuse. They are a blank space that tends to wash out the vividness of what is around them and should be used with caution.
- **Describe judiciously.** Many of us learned the lesson from grade school that when writing a story, one ought to show and not tell. This is only partly true. One should show crucial images with vividness. One can intentionally use vagueness for parts of the sermon that are less central to the message.

A final consideration when crafting the word picture is distance. When the preacher is describing an experience, exactly how close and personal does the preacher want to make the scene? Should the angle of the aperture remain relatively wide, such that it captures a broad view? Or should it zoom in on an experience? This consideration can be pastoral. If we take the example of my sermon following the Fourth of July shooting, there may be compelling reasons for widening and narrowing the aperture. It may be impactful to focus narrowly on a heroic act, or the ways that a member of the community facilitated healing after the event, both of which will impress such a moment into consciousness. At the same time, it may be sound pastoral strategy to avoid a narrow aperture focused on images of violence. Detailing bullets puncturing flesh could potentially open fresh or unresolved pain. Generally, a helpful rule is to ask whether the suggested description facilitates or distracts from the emotional movement of the sermon, which requires empathetic imagining and connection to the community.

Using vivid language is akin to blowing on the coals of the sermon. What looked cold and ashen suddenly bursts into flame. The imagery finds heat and movement in the mind of the receiver, fostering the gathered community's connection with the issue. With senses and emotions activated, the community is plunged into the scene—it is alive in them, and they are living in it. As the preacher draws folks toward the heart of the sermon, they feel invested in and connected to the message; they are awake to the stories being shared.

Put simply, vivid language is a powerful tool. It allows the preacher to picture another world and invite folks to imagine something new. It gives words life and power, and it prevents the sermon from becoming, in the words of Emerson, merely spectral.

Structuring the Sermon

There are a great variety of approaches to the sermon's form. The movement in the 1970s and 1980s known as the New Homiletic expended significant effort reflecting on and developing sermon structures. Books dedicated to anthologizing sermon forms have also sprung up, such as Dr. Ronald J. Allen's *Patterns of Preaching* and Thomas G. Long and Cornelius Plantinga's *A Chorus of Witnesses*. These works chart dozens of different structures and show what they look like through sample sermons.

In this section, I will not be detailing dozens of approaches, nor will I outline the history of sermon forms. Instead, my aim is simpler: to explore a well-known structure and show the ways it can be primed to express emotion and passion. This approach—often called narrative preaching—is especially attuned to producing and sustaining tension. When it is paired with awareness of the dynamics of pathos in the sermon, it can produce a powerful emotional result. To be clear, narrative preaching is not the only form that can express emotion. However, it is a tried-and-true one. Understanding and applying its basic principles are especially helpful for the passionate preacher.

The Narrative Sermon

Narrative preaching was developed through reflection on the most basic element of what a sermon is: a movement of words through time. In *The Homiletical Beat*, Eugene Lowry offers music as a metaphor for preaching. As the author admits, this has partly to do with the fact that he is a jazz musician. But he also argues that sermons are like music because both happen in time. There is a beginning, a middle, and an end. The music builds note upon note, chord upon chord, line upon line. The sermon builds word upon word, sentence upon sentence, movement upon movement. In this way, sermons are a process of building upon what has come before. Unlike, say, a visual image, this gives sermons the capacity to develop, to crest, to peak. And then, when they arrive at their end, they share with music a transient quality: They disappear into the air. There is no lasting artifact left, except, perhaps, for a musical score or a manuscript.

In everyday discussion, sermons are not often thought of in terms of movement. We might imagine a congregant who meets their preacher during the week and is curious about the sermon. They might ask something along the lines of, "What is the sermon you are working on about?" or perhaps, "What is the takeaway?" Often, when the preacher tries to deliver a statement that captures the sermon in a few lines, it sounds paltry in comparison with the preaching event. The statement "The sermon is about X" gives the impression that a sermon is a static form, as though one can have a high-level overview and then zoom in on particular details. It would be quite a different prospect, and more accurate to what Lowry describes, to think of it in terms of a novel, journey, or musical score. Instead of asking, "What's the main idea of the sermon?" the question would be, "Where does the sermon start, and where does it go?" Or rather than "What's the thesis?" the question would be, "What happens?" These questions reframe the sermon in terms of narrative movement through time.

When the sermon is understood in terms of its temporal dimension, a basic question follows: What makes the sermon compelling enough to command focus during that slice of time? Attention is not a given; the mind of the receiver can easily disembark. This has probably always been true, but it is especially pressing in the modern attention economy, which primes people to focus only on the next most exciting thing. To avoid losing folks, sermons need to be thoughtfully organized and give the sermon's receivers reasons to stay tuned in. For Lowry, the most powerful reason people stay focused is tension. There must be a built in tension that anchors focus on that movement of words through time, a stoking of suspense that tugs the receiver along until the sermon reaches its conclusion. This is why Lowry frames the sermon as a problem that moves toward a solution, an itch that moves toward a scratch, or an ambiguity that moves toward a resolution. This tensive quality forms the basic character of the narrative sermon.

Lowry first developed this dynamic in his groundbreaking work *The Homiletical Plot*, in which he explained the narrative structure as a series of movements in the sermon—what has come to be known as the Lowry Loop. The first movement is to take a commonly held belief or idea and to upset its equilibrium, the second is to analyze the discrepancy or tension, the third is to provide a clue to its resolution, the fourth is to experience the good news of its resolution, and the fifth is to analyze consequences. Since the publication of his first book, Lowry and others have refined, changed, expanded, and simplified these individual elements. For our purposes, I would like to reduce the form to its simplest components. We will rearticulate the Lowry Loop as a V-shaped sermon, similarly to Dr. O. Wesley Allen Jr. in *Determining the Form*. We can look at the first arm of the V of the sermon as a descent into a problem, the middle point as a hinge in which we experience a reversal that allows us to understand the situation anew, and the second arm as the experience of resolution.

The specific elements of narrative are less important than this overall three-part frame. What is needed is the buildup of tension or suspense, the disclosure of its solution, and the resolution of the tension.

The image of the V is imperfect, for it implies that both problem and solution receive an equal allotment of time in the narrative sermon. Actually, the disclosure of the solution occurs late in the structure because once it happens, the reason to stay tuned in dissipates. The solution cannot happen too early if the sermon is to maintain the tensive quality that commands interest.

The Pathos of the Narrative Form. Lowry's discussion of the narrative structure primarily centers on the sermon's logic, its logos. One might expect him to also tie it to pathos, as tension is a felt experience. However, Lowry does not explicitly reflect on the emotional experiences that attend to the sermon's problem and solution. For instance, I might state the problem of the sermon as "self-righteous politics are amplifying division," which could be a solid problem for a narrative sermon to address. I can imagine the reasons one might give for why this is troubling, including the flourishing of nasty rhetoric among neighbors and the tearing apart of families. But there is further interrogation that could happen here that would deepen the preaching experience. Is the preacher going to emphasize lament and grief for this condition? Or are they going to focus on the anger people harbor? What about desperation? Despair? Resentment, or even hatred? Many emotional components could underpin this sermon's problem and solution. The preacher needs to choose and thoughtfully cultivate the emotion if it is going to drive the narrative sermon.

So, how exactly does the narrative sermon organize the emotional experience?

Narrative structure applied to emotions is the transition from one emotional state to another. I may be feeling celebratory, only to have a distressing piece of news arrive. In this case, I move from one feeling state (celebratory joy) to another feeling state (worry or anxiety). Or perhaps I am feeling very little, and then I receive news that my friend's family was in a terrible accident. I am overwhelmed with worry. I then learn that everyone left it unscathed; my heart fills with relief and gratitude, and I move from feeling neutral to a negative emotion to a positive one.

The variety of emotional combinations are endless. We may move from feeling to not feeling and back again: from anxiety to joy, hope to outrage, wonder to love, fear to despair. The narrative sermon that makes use of emotion will intentionally craft a transition between feeling states, generally an undesirable emotional state to a desirable one, wherein the moment of transition is used as the sermon's hinge. This is what Lowry called the *clue to resolution*, or what I am calling the bottom of the V. For a pathos-focused sermon, this is the moment when the feeling structure changes.

Dr. Frank A. Thomas writes thoughtfully about this moment in *They Like to Never Quit Praisin' God*, his masterful exploration of preaching in the Black church. For Thomas, the skillful use of emotion in the sermon is necessarily tethered to reversal, inversion, and dramatic change. As he puts it, "Any preacher who would attend to emotional process must give careful thought to paradox, paradoxical intention, or . . . reversals." What he calls "deliberate disappointment" is when the preacher intentionally misleads the congregation: The preacher may unpack an experience of despair, leading the congregation deeply into heartbreak. At the point of the sermon's hinge, the preacher performs a bait and switch and suddenly the sermon changes course, and something hopeful is offered that countermands the despair. For Thomas, it is this reversal that leads to fresh encounter. Rarely will a masterful sermon simply present an emotional experience without a reversal. Instead, the preacher will engage the emotion through its movement and transformation, its arrival and transition.

This requires the tug of suspense. The emotion that exists before the hinge, before the bottom of the V, needs to be a taut rope—but it can be easy to let that rope go slack. Let us imagine an emotion the preacher intends to change once they arrive at reversal. The emotion starts out strong and is clearly embodied in the sermon's first segment, but an element is included that digresses from the emotional thrust. It relates intellectually to the sermon topic but provokes a different feeling experience in the receiver, and so the rope slackens. The community members may stay engaged because of the insight, but the emotional experience of that first movement no longer holds them. When the preacher arrives at the reversal, the community finds the resolution less compelling because the pathos of the sermon got lost in an eddy or meander. The emotional rope must hold through each element of the sermon if the sermon is going to maintain cohesive force. Once the transition occurs and the emotional context is reversed or changed, the emotion on the other side of the hinge also needs to compel, perhaps even more strongly. I think of this part of the sermon as a relentless tug toward the resolution.

Does this mean there is no room for intellectual discussion in the sermon? Does this mean that to create suspense, the whole sermon must be driven by emotionally provocative stories? As mentioned in the previous section, concrete language is preferable for building emotional power. At the same time, philosophical and theological elements can be included if they contribute to the growing sense of crisis (or resolution) in the sermon. This is the key concern for movements within a narrative frame—it is not a question of whether they are abstract or concrete, theology or story, but whether they compound an emotional experience and thereby inject or resolve tension in the plot.

Compounding an emotional experience can sound more heavy-handed than it needs to be. There is a bit on *Saturday Night Live* from many years ago called "Debbie Downer." The titular character, played deftly by Rachel Dratch, embodies a despairing view of the world—every time someone says something uplifting, she counters it with a dire fact or statistic. Usually, the things she says are non sequiturs. For Debbie Downer, no birthday party is complete without a description of famine, pet loss, and hurricane damage. The amalgam of dreadful, unrelated details is so over the top, it's cartoonish.

This is not the shape the sermon's pathos should take. Rather than piling on many unrelated elements that are held together only through shared feeling, the sermon's parts must be joined by a cogent, logical structure. The movements strike chords that lead people to experience the emotion, but these are relevant to the sermon's logical progression and therefore do not appear gratuitous or unjustified.

The emotion of the resolution must also relate to the logical progression of the sermon. It must be organic to the problem the sermon introduced, rather than a disconnected hope that has not been earned. Simply saying something like "Faith solves all problems," or "This is why we need beloved community" when there is no explanation or evidence will ring false. This is a time to be especially cautious of clichés. Sometimes preachers fall back on familiar tropes and platitudes to resolve the tension; I have heard preachers pluck statements from ancient texts or contemporary discussions whose meaning was established at some other time, in some other context. The preacher assumed its translatability would resolve the tension produced in the sermon. Instead, it sounded as though the preacher skimped on their homework. For the sermon to be convincing, the preacher needs to think and feel their way to a resolution. Rarely does this mean that a resolution can simply be plucked from another source.

How does one create and sustain emotional tension in a specific movement of the sermon? The answer is that the preacher must articulate the emotion as fully as possible as they craft the sermon. The words that capture the emotion of either the problem or the solution must then be threaded through each of the movements. I call these *words of poignancy*: moments that sink into the feeling structure of the sermon. For instance, in one recent sermon, some of these words of poignancy are: *desperate*, *pain*, *punishing*, *terrible*; and *bright*, *flash*, *new*, *hope*. Sometimes these words come at the crest of a particular movement or element, allowing for a brief buildup, peak, and pause. When the preacher delivers words of poignancy, they can be offered with a spark of embodied emotion. We will discuss the embodiment of emotion thoroughly in the next chapter. The point here is to name that these words, chords, and poignant moments must make an appearance in each movement to create the emotional tension that drives the sermon. Doing so holds the emotional rope taut as the preacher moves through the segment.

Bright, Ambiguous, and Problematic Emotions. The logical structure of the narrative sermon, its logos, moves from problem to solution. The emotional structure, its pathos, mirrors this progression. The most basic way that the logos and pathos fit together is when the sermon moves from worry or dismay (pathos) for the problem (logos) to relief, joy, or celebration (pathos) for the solution (logos). Thus, the problem will entail an undesirable emotional experience, while the solution will tend to feature a desirable one. There is no hard-and-fast rule for which emotions will be paired together; that decision depends on the content of the sermon and the emotions provoked. For example, one may feel rage for an instance of hate speech in the community and hope for the way that the community showed up to counter it. One might find that same rage paired with joy because the culprit came forward and repented. Some emotions easily fit more together, but I do not wish to impose any artificial rules about these pairings. Depending on the content of the logical structure, the emotional pairing will change.

But this is only part of the story. The homiletical move is also more nuanced than a simple transition from negative or undesirable emotions to positive or desirable ones. The discussion of emotional movement can give a false impression that ending with a desirable emotional experience equates with shallow cheerfulness. Such cheerfulness could wash out the reality of suffering, denying the severity of pain as well as the ongoing reality of suffering that cannot be resolved with a twenty-minute sermon. But skillful emotional transition does not mean glib denial of pain. Rather, it is a pastoral holding and hope that is realistic to the situation. Perhaps the preacher moves from grief over loss and tragedy to a hope that the community can bear witness and offer comfort. Here, the pain is not neatly resolved but held tenderly with compassion. The gathered community will experience such a move as more profound, as realistic holding in the midst of suffering strikes deeper chords of recognition and hope.

The homiletical move is also more nuanced than a simple transition from undesirable to desirable because bright emotions such as joy or hope, ambiguous emotions such as anger and grief, and problematic emotions such as hatred and contempt unfold in unique ways. Each has an idiosyncratic structure, which means that each emotion will require unique treatment to have impact.

Let's start with bright emotions, which are often the ones we choose to move toward in a sermon: joy, love, hope, or wonder. At first glance, it can seem that these emotions are easy to preach. Who doesn't want to experience a hopeful or joyful feeling? But these emotions can be surprisingly difficult to induce and sustain in a sermon because they tend to lack enough substance to make them convincing. For instance, producing a sermon that centers on hope without focusing on the movement *toward* hope is unlikely to compel. It is far more effective and convincing to produce hope from bleak experiences. The preacher is not spouting sunny optimism but rather a hard-won knowledge that suffering will not prevail. Folks find this compelling in part because it resonates with everyday realities plagued by suffering, and in part because it gives the bright feelings depth. Without implying their absence or lack, bright feelings can feel cheap.

This creates a need for transitional movement. For instance, despair turns on a hinge that leads to hope. Sorrow, to joy. Apathy, to wonder. The resulting complexity anchors the bright emotion in lived experience, and the bright emotion itself takes on a new hue. For the receivers, the bright emotion at the end of the sermon retains complexity, marked by the memory of the journey that evoked it.

I am taken with this quotation from *The Journals of Father Alexander Schmemann 1973-1983* on this point: "The knowledge of the fallen world does not kill joy, which emanates in this world always, constantly, as a bright sorrow." The idea of joy as bright sorrow moves the emotion from the realm of superfluity to profundity, accommodating the depth of human experience and anchoring the emotional experience in the heart. It also acknowledges the pain and difficulty that cannot be neatly solved or given closure with any given sermon.

Ambiguous emotions such as rage and lament require a different treatment. These emotions are engaged well when they have surprising complexity and subtle reversal. For instance, prophetic anger is not the same anger as feral rage or bitter regret. Instead, prophetic anger contains within it the demand for change. Its motivating force is the conviction that certain realities—indifference and callousness that cause groups to live with deprivation, injury, destruction, and violence—could be otherwise. Expressing outrage for these conditions implies that another world is possible. The skillful preacher will lift the brokenness that provokes anger, and then they will surface the kernel that yearns for another world, another possibility. This kernel does not live apart from the anger but is instead implicit within it.

The movement of prophetic anger is a careful unpacking of its nuance. It refuses to be satisfied with lashing out and insists instead on change and commitment. The experience of outrage thus contains hope for a different world, or perhaps love as a social conviction, or even joy at the impermanence of structures that oppress and degrade.

Lament is another ambiguous emotion, one with its own complex structure. Like prophetic anger, it is a negative feeling that carries a brighter one within it. Here, the preacher—figuratively or literally—weeps for a world that could be but is not. That tenderness, that heartache, evokes a powerful hope for a different outcome. When lament enters the sermon, it contains both sadness and possibility. And as if this were not sufficient, it also contains a belligerent kernel. The shedding of tears is also the statement of an emphatic "Enough!" This is not demure sadness or a despair that causes retreat into solitude. Instead, it is the forceful insertion of one's pain into public spaces. The decorum of many settings opposes such expressions, while lament rends the barriers of social acceptability. In this way, lament contains sadness and yearning but also aggressive persistence. It is a sadness that refuses to be denied.

I have found this mixture of emotion to be powerful and difficult to engage in the homily. With outrage, people are energized. With lament, people are often introspective and somewhat stung by the pain, even when lament surfaces hope or joy for another possibility. Spaces that help people discuss and process the emotion of a lament sermon can be a helpful tool.

The transitional movement within ambiguous emotions is internal to the emotion itself. To the extent possible, the preacher separates the injury of the offense from the determination to find a different possibility, allowing for the emotion to split into two parts that turn on a hinge. Generally, the preacher first narrows the frame to the offending elements as the sermon descends the first arm of the V. Then, after the hinge, the preacher focuses on yearning for a different possibility. Anger or sadness will remain, but so will a hope, or joy, or tenderness that tugs the worshipper toward a different possibility. Just as joy becomes bright sorrow, anger and lament end as aggrieved hope. This psychological nuance is what causes it to catch in consciousness and motivates the community members to seek change in their lives and their world.

The last cluster of emotions, including hatred, resentment, and contempt, is the most difficult if not distressing—perhaps so much so that these emotions do not belong in the sermon at all. How one responsibly includes them is a controversial question, or at least it should be. Unfortunately, these emotions have been and are too often weaponized in sermons that promote harmful messages. For the progressive preacher, these emotions must be carefully framed if they appear at all.

My approach to preaching is to unravel, diminish, or reverse these feelings; I generally believe they should have little motivating force in the context of the sermon. Considering the deeply problematic history of their use, it is better to collapse them.

Interestingly, the Gospels contain a story about how to diminish these feelings, Jesus's Parable of the Good Samaritan. Here, Jesus confronts the crowd with its negative stereotypes of Samaritans, which would have reminded his listeners of their disdain for them. But when Jesus tells of the Samaritan doing a praiseworthy act, he challenges their contempt and lays the groundwork for transforming that undesirable emotional association. While the gathered crowd may have felt comfort with the problematic emotional connotations, Jesus intentionally disorients them, upsetting their capacity to maintain these associations and inviting them to move beyond resentment and hatred.

This is a crucial option for a sermon that treats this problematic cluster of emotional experiences. The sermon descends into contempt and resentment and then pivots on the hearer's misappraisal of the situation, a chastising movement that can be difficult to make in a sermon. Members are unlikely to receive chastisement without a solid relationship with the preacher. Even then, including oneself within the critique is a smart choice.

Another option for handling these negative feelings was developed by Professor Brent A. Strawn, who writes in *Honest to God Preaching* about the tradition of imprecatory prayer in the Hebrew scriptures. Though less attended to by many modern religious groups, these are prayers that vent hatred at the forces that injure and oppress. As Strawn speculates, these prayers were often made in the context of great suffering and pain. The psalmist begs for an enemy's destruction while weeping for the wounded. There is a raw candor here, a naked struggle with both pain and hatred. It begs the question: In the context of deep injury, what is one to do with one's contempt? Perhaps being honest is a start. Strawn links this need for honesty with trauma recovery, where established therapies create a safe container for complicated emotional responses. Such permission for honest expression allows for the healing process to begin, rather than submerging and ignoring the emotion.

Strawn argues the same can be said for the imprecatory impulse. Finding a safe space to get real about one's contempt, resentment, and hatred can stop them from coming out sideways. Indeed, sometimes this honesty lessens the impulse and allows one to reorient one's life, holding complicated feelings in good faith. In the context of the sermon, naming such emotions can alleviate them and lessen their force. The homiletical movement here is the lessening or diminishment of the problematic emotion by grappling with it honestly, which allows the preacher to pivot toward a broader, more generous expression when the sermon reaches its hinge.

Broadening Narrative Structure

This section has discussed narrative structure as the organizing dynamic of the passionate sermon, but is narrative always the best way to frame sermon structure? Critics outside of the homiletic world have challenged what they call the *tyranny of narrative.* These writers argue that forcing every message or experience into a narrative form is limiting, especially with the narrative form I am advocating here, which follows a singular buildup and release of tension. As these theorists note, excellent literature only sometimes follows that pattern; life follows it even less frequently. And so, rather than a straight line that intensifies and releases conflict, there are dozens if not hundreds of forms that can be leveraged, some of which are detailed in Jane Alison's *Meander, Spiral, Explode.* The passionate preacher would do well to consider the rules of the narrative form and the opportunities to break with it.

The narrative sermon is, for me, a reliable structure to fall back on. But I often find myself ordering the sermon in different ways. Sometimes intentionally, sometimes intuitively, I sense a different form will provide a better vehicle. These alternative structures do not abandon but rather rework the principles of tension and release. Here are a few ways that this can be done—forms to which I have given my own spin, and ones that work especially well with the pathos-driven sermon:

- **The sawtooth sermon.** This form imagines the sermon as a series of ridges. Each one builds tension and then releases it before moving on to the next ridge. The emotional tension and emotional resolution are the same in each movement or anecdote, binding the sermon into a cohesive whole. For instance, if the tension is the buildup of despair, the solution in each could be the crest of joy.

- **The scorpions-in-a-box sermon.** This sermon is a battle between two theologies, ideologies, or concepts. Both seem equally strong. Perhaps it is obvious which one you want to win, perhaps not. Perhaps one delivers the final sting, or they both die because they need to. Perhaps they reach a truce. Perhaps the final move is to smash the box and set them free. The tension is the bad feeling generated by the conflict. The emotional solution is the salve that heals the tension.
- **The yo-yo sermon.** This sermon begins with the solution in hand. But rather than a deductive sermon that tells the audience what the argument will be, it then casts the solution far away. It "loses" the solution. There is no obvious connection between the middle movements and the first movement, leaving folks to wonder how one could find their way back to the solution. Only at the end does the congregation achieve clarity as the solution comes firmly back in hand.

What the reader will notice is that each form still includes principles of the narrative sermon. While these forms are not working along a single trajectory and piling on undesirable feelings until they are resolved, the tension and release are still there, allowing for an emotionally satisfying experience while offering a different structure or form. This range of alternatives can be freeing for preachers who navigate a wide range of texts, issues, ideas, stories, and needs. They give latitude not to force but to experiment. And for congregation members who come every week, there will be something refreshing in the varied sermon structure. After all, few want to experience the same song every time they turn on the radio—but they still want to feel something.

5

ONCE MORE, WITH FEELING: DELIVERING THE PASSIONATE SERMON

I was never musical. My talent extends to singing hymns under my breath on Sunday and the occasional "Happy Birthday" song. But I went to a high school that had a large student orchestra. I would sometimes pass the performance room in the hallway, listening to the students give their best. I would peek into the door that had been propped open, watching the chaos of instruments that obscured serious faces intent on getting the notes right. Often, the students would be so focused on the task that they would leave out another important ingredient, at which point the teacher would say to the students: "Okay, that was good, but let's take it from the top. Once more, with feeling!"

For the passionate sermon, this is where we preachers face the music. The sermon may have a brilliant spark and a great structure—it may use empathy and language to craft a powerful message—but if the preacher is unable to embody the emotional experience, the outcome will be underwhelming. This chapter thus explores the process of embodiment and delivery. It uses theories of affect transmission to understand how and why emotions are shared within crowds, surveys approaches to acting and embodiment that facilitate emotional communication in the preaching moment, and relies on various rhetorical techniques to explore the use of crescendo and climax in preaching. When these elements are harmonized, the sermon finds feeling and force.

A Theory of Emotional Transmission

The transmission or sharing of emotions in crowds is a well-known phenomenon that theorist Anna Gibbs describes memorably in "Contagious Feelings": "Bodies can catch feelings as easily as catch fire: affect leaps from one body to another, evoking tenderness, inciting shame, igniting rage, exciting fear—in short, communicable affect can inflame nerves and muscles in a conflagration of every conceivable kind of passion." While most of us have experienced this kind of emotional transmission—a feeling shared among a crowd or group—it is a curiosity as to why or how it occurs. Emotions are often thought to be deeply interior states. My own experience of loss, for instance, is not only private but one that I may struggle to articulate for others. So how is it that emotions can extend from one person to the next seemingly without effort or orchestration?

As it turns out, some have pondered these questions, and their findings are insightful for passionate preachers. Passionate preaching is nothing more nor less than affect transmission—the sharing of an emotional experience in a gathered community.

Teresa Brennan's book *The Transmission of Affect* unpacks the ways that affect is shared between people. She asks, "Is there anyone who has not, at least once, walked into the room and 'felt the atmosphere'?" Her work attempts to explain why so many answer in the affirmative and follows the investigations of psychoanalysis, psychology, and social psychology to find answers. According to Brennan, these schools of thought have only sometimes answered the question fruitfully. Often, they have conceived of emotions as internal states that are selectively exposed to others. While theorists have written extensively about the ways people's identities are socially produced, they have sometimes sheltered feelings as the last bastion of individualism and insisted on the interiority and privacy of emotions. Other theorists have noted the fact that transmission occurs but failed to clarify why or how. This lack of insight, Brennan argues, is strange given the prevalence of the social exchange of emotion. The atmosphere of a crowd can be palpable, tangible. It can move from the outside in, reshaping the felt experience of the individuals who encounter it and the crowd that generates it.

Brennan theorizes emotional exchange in terms of speech and body. She calls this an *alphabet of the flesh* expressed in physical gesture and vocality. Such an alphabet is written with a variety of subtle cues. The vehicle is embodiment itself, with all the fullness the word entails. When someone comes into a room and senses a tense atmosphere, they may be reading any number of understated bodily signals: Certain people are not making eye contact. Others are hunching their shoulders. Someone's brow is furrowed. Many are wearing a frown, while one person seems to be smiling uncomfortably. Limbs are crossed. One person is wide-eyed and keeps looking to the side. Sentences are clipped and short, as though people are measuring what to say. Breathing is shallow. The person who enters the room does not necessarily name any of these things. Instead, they start to feel their gut clench, their heart race, their brows knit together. They have a wish to leave but do not have the language for why. Any number of signals communicate emotion through such an experience, and these cues are exchanged through the totality of bodily expressions, many of them subtle and below the conscious level.

These emotions may also be transmitted into speech, which can happen in subtle or unconscious ways. When my friend was young, his parent would sometimes share how her day went. She would not say she had a good or bad day; instead, she would say she had a good day or a "good day." The first of these was genuine. The other meant she was unhappy with something, often something my friend had done or failed to do. He and his siblings came to notice the difference in her subtle inflection. The "good day" comment—the one that heralded bad news—always sounded effortful. While subtle, it was nonetheless a way that affective experience imprinted itself in speech.

The body and its emotions translate into language whether or not the words of the speaker align with them. As Brennan poetically puts it, "The different alphabets of the flesh could be aligned in such a way that life [is] released from one order into another." In other words, our bodies may communicate themselves in ways that elude our conscious intentions and notice.

Here, the experience of affect transmission is the reading of another's emotion through the totality of embodied cues. Like a sixth sense, people read what others are feeling. Of course, thinking of it as a sense, as a faculty that people possess, does not mean it never fails. People sometimes bungle interactions; they misread bodily cues. On more than one occasion, I have misunderstood emotional contexts and said something unfortunate. Such misunderstandings are commonplace, but the surprising frequency of affective transmission speaks to its power. Many preachers wield this skill intuitively, while those who neglect it find the impact of their preaching diminished.

Mastering emotional communication in the context of the sermon is challenging. If we were speaking of narrative organization, conceptual clarity, and word choice, we could submit a manuscript to a colleague who could take out their red pen, mark up the text, and send it back. Once those errors were corrected and the language clarified, the preacher would have a better chance of expressing intent. Unfortunately, this is not the case with emotional transmission. We are talking about subtle, often unconscious signals that either facilitate or diminish the emotional experience of the receiver. This is why, despite valiant attempts to mask certain affects, preachers may nonetheless receive feedback about their nervousness, for example. The subtle embodied cues speak for themselves. What is required for effective emotional transmission in the pulpit is the convincing embodied performance of the feeling, an ability to experience and embody the emotion in the pulpit in a persuasive way.

In *The Managed Heart*, Arlie Hochschild develops helpful categories for understanding the performance of emotion. She is interested in the ways people in the corporate world manage their emotional experiences, which requires, for instance, the effort to display happiness or compassion in jobs that demand it. As with an actor onstage, such emotions are performed or enacted through different methods. Surface acting, she says, highlights the disconnect between presentation and internal experience. A store clerk may smile and feign interest in a new washing machine, even though her internal experience is boredom. A nurse might use a soothing tone with an irritable patient, even though his internal emotion is anxiety. In either case, the external presentation is different from the internal experience. Simply put, the person is faking it. Likely, the worker is aware of the disconnect because of the sheer effort or labor required to produce an incongruous emotional expression.

Deep acting, in contrast, pertains to the ways participants convince themselves they have a particular feeling. Here, the store clerk attempts to erase the disconnect between presentation and internal experience. She might try to convince herself the merchandise is exciting, even when she does not feel that way. The nurse similarly convinces himself that he possesses the appropriate emotion. He might say to himself, "I know it may seem like I am anxious, but I really do care about this patient." Such exercises used to shift feeling states can entail cognitive or bodily acting techniques. The store clerk might utilize phrases to talk herself into excitement about the product, which would be a cognitive exercise. Alternatively, the nurse may use slow, steady breaths to calm his anxiety, which would be a physical technique. These deep-acting techniques attempt to manage an emotional disconnect by closing the gap between personal experience and professional presentation. They dismiss or diminish the undesirable emotion in favor of one that is acceptable for the context in an attempt to truly feel that emotion rather than simply mimic or fake it.

The preacher may experience external and internal obstacles to inhabiting emotion in the pulpit. Often, this is not because the emotion is insincere but because it requires effort to effectively inhabit, experience, and demonstrate. Especially in the pulpit, where nerves, distractions, and other worries can overcome the preacher, performance or acting techniques may be required to effectively express emotions. Such acting cannot simply be forced surface presentation; the subtleties of body and speech may betray the preacher. They may transmit unintentional affect (such as anxiety) even while attempting to project another emotion (such as joy). Thus, it is crucial that the preacher feels the commanding emotion of the passionate sermon even if they must talk themselves into it or use other deep-acting techniques to provoke the emotion. To the extent that the preacher can imagine and inhabit that emotion, they will be more likely to enliven it for members through the array of embodied cues.

Exercise: Naming Emotion in a Recent Sermon

Think about the last sermon you gave. What emotions did it express? Choose one and take some time to journal in response to the following questions: What did it feel like when I expressed that emotion in the pulpit? Where did it arise in my body? How long was I able to sustain it? Did anything external distract or diminish the emotional experience? Were there any internal experiences that diminished the emotion? Were there parts of the sermon that especially provoked the feeling? What were they, and why did they do so? Write down any insights about what distracted from and what facilitated emotional expression.

There is a further limitation to the ability to express emotions in the sermon. The preacher may experience personal psychological blocks not only to the performance but also to the internal experience of emotions. In that case, the emotions can only be accessed through surface acting because they cannot be genuinely inhabited. Like a switch, the internal experience of the emotion is turned off. The pathos of the sermon will therefore be less convincing. In such cases, the preacher would do well to avail themselves of therapeutic methods that facilitate connection and expression of emotion.

I realize this part of passionate preaching moves the conversation beyond the realm of a how-to manual and treads realms of personal introspection that could require months if not years to explore. Nonetheless, such psychic curiosity is important if a preacher wishes to be effective. While the conversation here will necessarily be abbreviated, I would like to offer one tool for exploring such emotional terrain.

Hilary Jacobs Hendel's *It's Not Always Depression* offers insight into the blocks that prevent people from inhabiting and expressing emotions. Her view is that core emotions are sometimes restrained by what she calls defenses and inhibitory emotions. I will offer a personal example of what this looks like.

I am someone who has struggled with the expression of grief. In my mid-twenties, I lost my first husband in an accident. The experience was so overwhelmingly intense that approaching the emotions felt like being flooded or drowned. Whenever I was close to expressing the grief, anxiety would surge because I believed the grief would be annihilating. To manage the anxiety, I would detach and go blank. The latter defense was what I came to associate with grief. When I attended therapy, it was in part because I did not understand why sadness felt so remote and inaccessible. I had gone through an enormously painful experience, yet I could barely access the emotions around it. From there on out, it was a slow process of discovering and thawing out for me.

Curiously, what I began to notice is that beneath the defense of detachment and the inhibitory anxiety, something living and vital was waiting to be expressed. I began to touch on my grief, slowly unpacking the experience of losing my husband. My ability to freely express emotions of sadness and grief became more fluid and, over time, more manageable. Instead of worrying that an experience of sorrow would swallow me, I came to trust that I could dip into that emotion and exit it as well. This capacity benefitted not only my personal life but also my abilities as a preacher. When appropriate, I could move to the edge of feelings of lament and grief and pull back. I could facilitate others' experiences without being consumed. The more I engaged, the more I could embody these emotions in the pulpit.

Exercise: Taking an Emotional Inventory

Take a journal or notebook. On one page, write down heavier emotions, including anger and sadness. Leave space under each emotion so that you can brainstorm. Now do the same on another page for lighter emotions, such as joy and love. Contemplate your experience with the heavy or negative emotional experiences. Are some harder to access than others? Why might that be? Notice both the emotions and beliefs that come up when you reach for these heavier experiences. Are you afraid of losing control or being swallowed by the emotion? Are there other feelings, such as anxiety, that accompany these emotions? What message did you receive while growing up about expressing them? How does it feel to express those emotions in private, or with a trusted friend versus in public? What defenses do you use to thwart emotions when they start to arise? Now, spend some time asking similar questions for the lighter emotions.

Note that work around deep-seated beliefs and expressions often takes time and effort. The point of this exercise is simply to bring awareness to some of the limitations the preacher may have. It may also become an invitation for further interior work.

As the preacher becomes more fluid with the expression of emotions, a certain muscle memory develops. The expression of grief, outrage, or joy comes more easily, and the preacher can dip in and out of them at will. As an allegory, one might think here of a person learning to drive. For a student driver, pulling up to a stop sign entails deep intention: remembering the difference between a rolling stop and a full stop, applying the brakes, counting out three seconds, looking for cars and pedestrians, and only then applying the gas. It is all highly conscious. Eventually, though, intentional effort disappears. One can drive from one part of town to another with no memory of the trip because it is fully engrained within unconscious muscle memory. The same is true for emotion and passionate expression. Once someone learns the dynamics of expressing emotions and is comfortable evoking them with speech, the effort disappears. But at first, it takes time and practice, and it requires getting specific about the ways the body communicates subtle emotional language.

Techniques for Effective Delivery

The totality of bodily expression, from breath to gesture to posture to gaze, betrays the emotions. Understanding this is the first step to the effective communication of emotion in the pulpit, but we also need more than this. Understanding *why* emotions are transmitted does not tell us how to generate, sustain, and communicate them.

For that, we need to turn to acting strategies that focus on embodiment and emotional transmission.

As a way into this conversation, let's start by analyzing two vignettes from a preaching workshop I led. The following are composites of participants who took the workshop and, as we will see, represent very different ways of inhabiting the pulpit.

> Thomas is a fifty-year-old white man with a mane of salt-and-pepper hair. He is about six-foot-two. He confided to the workshop participants earlier that he played college football, and then went on to teach math. Thomas now plans on ministry in the parish. His shoulders are broad, and he often wears a kind, gentle expression. He has little formal public speaking experience besides his middle-school math classroom. When he approaches the metal lectern, I must remind him to adjust the height so he can see his notes. He nervously shuffles the pages, coughs, glances up at the group, and then quickly looks away. The lectern is a tiny thing compared to his presence, and yet he appears dwarfed by it. He stands too far behind it, causing him to awkwardly reach his hands far in front of him to move the pages. When he is not turning pages, he holds his hands and fidgets. During his sermon, he rarely makes eye contact. His breath is shallow. He rushes through the pages of his manuscript, which causes him to trip over several words. The end of each sentence falls off, so it is difficult to hear what he is saying. There is an almost apologetic look on Thomas's face throughout the sermon. Little to no variation exists in his tone. His final sentence trails off as he looks down at his notes. He hurries away from the pulpit.

> Corrine is a thirty-five-year-old Hispanic woman, with long, slick black hair pulled into a braid. She is about

> five-foot-six. She is trained as a lawyer and has about a decade of public speaking experience in which she needed to be forthright and persuasive. Upon arriving at the lectern, she immediately adjusts its height to meet her smaller frame, grips both sides, and takes a moment to look out over the assembled participants. She appears to be in complete control of the pulpit; it is a tool for her use. Deliberate gestures match the rise and fall of emotion in her speech. Each line is punctuated forcefully. Her breath is steady, and her facial expressions vary depending on the emotion she is communicating. Her pace is even, though when she hits appropriate moments in her sermon, the speed and volume increase. The final line of her sermon ends on a hard stop. She stands for a moment in the pulpit, making eye contact with the participants. Only then does she leave the lectern.

Preaching theory can be highly attuned to the words of the sermon manuscript, and it can attend to theology, language, structure, and story. But what is important to notice here is that the vignettes above say nothing of the manuscript. They are indifferent to elements of content, and yet they say everything about the effectiveness of the preacher.

This is because a sermon is not black marks on white paper. A sermon is breath, movement, gesture, enunciation, pause, pace, volume, expression, and silence. It is the difference between an English class reading a text by Shakespeare and an acting class that performs a Shakespearean drama. As I hope our previous attention to language, theology, and sermon structure makes clear, this is not to say that elements of content and form are irrelevant. They are crucial. But in a discipline that has sometimes underestimated sermon delivery in favor of homiletic content, it is important to press the issue. Preaching is not a manuscript; it is an event.

The other thing to notice is that the descriptions of Thomas and Corrine do not explore emotions in delivery or point out elements of passionate expression. Instead, they highlight basic observations about what makes preaching effective: the principles of self-assurance, openness, and engagement with those who are present. These qualities communicate that the preacher is solidly grounded in their authority and empathetic connection. It is a way of communicating with the body: *I am confident in what I need to share with you, and you are valuable to me. This message is for you.* These two sentiments of authority and empathy are the baseline for the effective sermon. When they wobble, they compromise every other purpose and emotion present in the sermon. If we are preaching a sermon that moves from despair to joy, neither will be effectively communicated without this baseline.

How do we move from Thomas's timidness and fumbling to Corrine's command and connection? One way to do so is to take it element by element. We can look at the contrast in eye contact, pace, variation of voice, breathing, facial expressions, etc. This approach can clarify what specific physical gestures communicate to the receivers: When the eyes are glued to the page, the message is that the preacher does not recognize or care about the gathered community or is unsure of their words. The preacher can communicate timidness and uncertainty about the message. Sustained eye contact, by contrast, communicates that the preacher values the people who are present. It suggests not simply, *This is the message*, but rather, *This is a message for* you.

Of course, preachers with different abilities find unique ways to connect; not all effective preachers will use eye contact. The point here is that breaking down physical elements bit by bit is one way to assist preachers, and when we are trying to achieve a particular effect, such as a powerful crescendo, it will be necessary to examine discrete elements.

At the same time, going letter by letter through the alphabet of the flesh can be overwhelming. By the time the preacher goes from *B* for *breathing* to *F* for *facial expression*—much less *P* for *pace*—the preacher is balancing a lot. Luckily for preachers, we can draw on acting strategies that bolster specific embodied experiences, emphasizing a single point of focus rather than multiple changes. The strategies need to be adapted; after all, they are designed to inhabit a particular character in a drama. However, they can be used for the purpose of embodied preaching to great effect.

Leading Center

In character acting, a leading center refers to a trait that grounds an interpretation of a character. For instance, a character who is avaricious might rub imaginary coins throughout the performance. An actor portraying an ideologically rigid character might lose the capacity to flex their joints. But this is more than a mere affectation, a quality that could be cast off without changing much about the performance. Instead, the leading center serves as an ongoing reminder of the personality the actor is attempting to project. Focusing on the rigidity of joints anchors and infuses the rest of the presentation, inflecting speech, response, and interaction.

When the preacher, rather than the actor, seeks to use the leading center, there are key differences. I do not think it is especially effective or helpful to cultivate affectation that is unnatural for the preacher. However, this exercise can be used to focus on a part of the body, an anchor point, that grounds the energetic intention the preacher wishes to project. During the rehearsal of the sermon, the preacher will draw their attention to the leading center. As the focus on it builds, the intention seeps deeper and deeper into demeanor and language. This energetic focus will have a physical effect. Observing oneself in the mirror or receiving feedback as one works on cultivating the leading center will show subtle but concrete physical changes. Imagining those changes, along with the leading center, during rehearsal and then before one enters the pulpit will help facilitate the effect. Ideally, doing so during the rehearsal will free the preacher in the preaching moment while still embodying the intention.

Personally, I have used three leading centers when preaching, each one offering a different effect. You are welcome to experiment with these and also to try new ones that fit your style.

- **Fire behind the eyes.** This leading center invites the preacher to imagine there is the light of a burning fire behind the eyes. If an independent observer were to describe this light, they would use adjectives such as *intense*, *forceful*, *focused*, *powerful*, and *determined*. This light collects the intensity of felt experience, drawing energy from deep within the body. Imagine that when you look out at those who are gathered, this fire is enticing others toward the light. This is an especially helpful leading center when the preacher receives feedback that their preaching lacks energy or commitment.
- **Open heart.** This leading center invites the preacher to imagine that the heart is undefended by skin, bone, or viscera. It is exposed to the gathered community, a thing of gentle vulnerability that is deeply receptive to the sorrow and pain of others. Its receptivity comes from the fact that you, too, have been wounded. If others were to perceive this open heart, they would describe it as *receptive*, *kind*, *gentle*, *patient*, and *compassionate*. Imagine that when you look at the congregation, your heart has a profound capacity to receive the pain others bring. This is an especially helpful leading center when the preacher receives feedback that their demeanor is overly intellectual, aloof, and disconnected.
- **Lead ball.** This leading center invites the preacher to imagine that there is a lead ball deep inside their core, just below the

> ribs. This is a place of weight and heft. It is heavy, so heavy that it anchors your feet to the floor. If others were to describe it, they would say it is *secure*, *grounded*, *settled*, and *stable*. Imagine that when you look at the congregation, this lead ball grounds the energy of the worship atmosphere. The anchor in the pit of your chest is so strong, it absorbs any anxious or restless energy in yourself or others. This leading center is especially helpful when the preacher feels nervous, unsettled, or disembodied.

These powerful tools can help the preacher embody a grounded, convicted, and relational preaching style. For many, using even one of these may be enough to create an effective pulpit presence.

Finding Emotion under the Words

Once the preacher feels confident with a leading center they may choose to experiment with another technique, which involves delivering words using different emotional intentions. It is the difference between reading a poem about sorrow and reading a poem with sorrow expressed in the body and voice.

Let's get specific and take a few lines of poetry from W. H. Auden. Readers have delivered "Funeral Blues" in very different ways, from ironic and overstated to a sincere expression of grief. Depending on the reader's interpretation, the delivery of the lines will sound very, very different. Let's focus on the final stanza of the poem:

> The stars are not wanted now; put out every one,
>
> Pack up the moon and dismantle the sun,
>
> Pour away the ocean and sweep up the wood;
>
> For nothing now can ever come to any good.

Consider delivering these lines with a variety of emotional intentions: biting sorrow for a lost love, mocking derisiveness for another's woe, anger at the impermanence of life, or a child laughingly tipping over toy blocks. As you deliver these lines with different emotions, notice the difference in emphasis, facial expression, posture, enunciation, and speed. The alphabet of the flesh should spell out something different in each instance.

For this technique to be effective, the preacher needs to understand the rhythm of emotion in speech. If it is to be natural, it cannot be overdone; there ought to be an ebb and flow to the underlying emotion. In other words, moments can express the emotional intention without turning every line into overwrought performance. Curiously, this restraint has the effect of amplifying the emotion rather than diminishing it. Pulling people again and again toward the emotion of the sermon will feel more compelling than relentless production of the same effect.

When delivering a particular part of the sermon, not every line will be accented with emotion. How does one know which lines to accent? Often, these lines become obvious through rehearsal. In a previous chapter, I called them moments of poignancy: words or lines that crystalize the underlying emotion of the message and perhaps express the culmination of an idea or story, the moment that packs the most punch. Let us look again at the lines from the Auden poem. For the purposes of this exercise, let's interpret them as an expression of sincere grief. Which of these lines renders grief most poignantly?

The answer is clear: The first three lines form a prelude to the last line. The idea is that one will do all these things—pack up the sun and put away the stars—*because* there is no good left in the world. Therefore, the last line is the clearest one to stress with a sorrowful tone.

What does it mean to use a sorrowful tone? It means understanding what happens to your voice, mouth, gestures, shoulders, eyebrows, forehead, chest, and throat in moments of lament. It means contemplating the following questions: When and how do tears start to form? What is the exact pitch of a word that is penetrated with grief? Where is your breath? What parts of the body tremble? What goes still? What happens to your eyebrows, chin, and lips? The questions do not need to end here, but they can start here. It is important to know these answers not intellectually but viscerally, in the body.

When lines with an emotional peak are threaded through the sermon, a wavelike rhythm develops. The preacher can do many things in the sermon, including teach, debate, explore, discuss, and converse. Sermons can include poetry, theology, and story. These elements do not need to be delivered with a dramatic, overblown, emotional tone. However, they will lead to moments of emotional potency when the commanding emotion of the sermon breaks through. Sometimes, this wavelike structure will lead to an emotional crescendo at the end, which is a powerful option for preaching. We will explore this shortly, though the wavelike structure of emotion in the sermon does not need to climax at the end to be effective. Instead, the rhythm can produce a powerful and complete effect on its own, which allows for the preacher to move toward a quiet, reflective ending rather than a thunderous one, if they choose.

Connectivity

Yet another issue in delivery is the question of connectivity. Jason Byassee addresses this question in his 2022 article "Preaching Weird," which is based on his interviews and work with Tetsuro Shigematsu, a stage magician who serves as a consultant to clergy, helping them improve their pulpit presence. Shigematsu uses metaphors for understanding what is happening in the preaching moment.

One is the metaphor of the glass tube, or the idea that certain habits place the speaker inside of a tube that removes them from the congregation. It is nonporous, separating the preacher into their own private world of theological pondering that happened earlier in the week. When the preacher is stuck inside the glass tube, it translates as distance, aloofness, and even coldness.

Shigematsu contrasts the aloof, distant speech of the sermon with other speech that happens during the service. When a member shares joy or sorrow, asks for a prayer from the congregation, or gives an unscripted testimony, the speech is of the moment. In other words, the very lack of preparation connects the speaker with the congregation. No notes or manuscripts or even forethought separate the speech of the person from the community. The congregation is right there with the person, especially when their request is accompanied by heartfelt emotional expression. How can the preacher's language function more like the person who is making the in-the-moment, unscripted request or statement to the congregation? How can the preacher break the glass tube that separates them from the congregation?

To address these questions, Byassee argues that the preacher should show up less prepared. While I appreciate the intention, I have witnessed lack of preparation go awry. The preacher attempts to be relatable by standing up and saying what is on their mind, but rather than relaxed and conversational, it comes off as lazy and unthoughtful. As author Clyde E. Fant puts it in *Preaching for Today*, "There is nothing more deadly to preaching than the person who can say nothing for thirty minutes, and knows it." Rather than advocate for lack of preparation, I suggest another option: reevaluating one's assumptions about the purpose of the sermon and what is happening in the preaching moment.

To explore this, I invite the reader to imagine two different scenarios. The first is a report delivered in a high school English class, which is anchored in the following assumptions: *I am being evaluated by someone based on the content of my speech*; *I must hew as closely as possible to my carefully crafted language to succeed*; *what's most important are the words in front of me*; *the audience is an instrument to me getting a better grade*. Now, consider a second scenario—the dynamics of a conversation with a close friend. *There is no one evaluating me*; *there are no words I must faithfully recite*; *the person in front of me is the only important thing in this moment*; *my language is just an instrument for connection*.

What should be clear is that the expectations of the high school report and the conversation with a friend are worlds apart. Unfortunately, many preachers treat the sermon more like the report than the conversation.

To embody connectivity, the preacher must know this truth in their bones: *What's real, and what's really important, are the people who are sitting right in front of me. The manuscript, notes, and preparation are all just tools to facilitate connection*. It is truly not important if particular points, language, or ideas come across. While the preacher knows the interpretations, descriptions, movements, and arguments of the sermon, nothing will be lost if those do not come off perfectly. *If I do not say the brilliant thing I crafted earlier in the week, that does not matter as long as I am facilitating connection*. The preacher should internally reaffirm this idea before the service starts. The more the preacher can embody that belief and rehearse it, the more they will project that connectivity to the congregation through the subtle signals that communicate below conscious thought.

What this means is the preacher needs to internalize the sermon so they can take leave of it, knowing what comes next even without reading the words. The point here is not a perfect rendition of the manuscript but the opposite: to be familiar enough with it that the preacher can easily depart from their page, attend to the congregation, perhaps riff off the text, and then return to the manuscript without it being obvious. This comfort is not mastered with lack of preparation but rather with more preparation. Only repetition and practice allow the preacher to achieve this mastery and ease. But when this preparation is paired with prioritizing connection to the congregation, this can generate an effective pulpit presence.

Rehearsal

Leading center, emotional accent, connectivity, and other techniques must be honed with rehearsal. When someone asks me the quickest way to improve their preaching, I always ask them: What is the amount of time spent composing the sermon versus the amount of time spent rehearsing it? I find people often give an enormous fraction to either writing or researching the sermon and only a tiny slice of time to practicing it. Sometimes preachers will polish it on the computer until the last minutes before the service. They then leave their office with a manuscript they have not delivered any part of. I urge a serious reevaluation of such habits. Preaching is an embodied event; it happens when one is behind the pulpit, not behind the computer. For this reason, one should attend to rehearsal. If the preacher sacrifices this rehearsal time, there will likely be stumbling and gaps, losing one's place, mispronounced words, and failed emotional connections—all of which distract from the preacher's intention.

So what exactly is the preacher doing as they rehearse? First, they are searching for language that might work for the written word but not for the spoken word. Preachers can look for signals that language is not prepared for speech—compound sentences, sentences with multiple subjects and verbs, and sentences that require more than a breath should all be simplified in the final manuscript. Likewise, words should fall within the vocabulary range that is typical for the speaker. Unfamiliar words, words that are difficult to pronounce, or words known only to the professorate at the preacher's divinity school should be excised. These elements reinforce the glass tube rather than break it. By the time the preacher brings the manuscript into the pulpit, it should look like something you don't want to hand to someone after the service. Think of it as a blunt tool to help you facilitate an event. Its destiny is the recycle bin.

It is a smart idea for the preacher to practice their sermon in front of a mirror—or, if the preacher has a visual impairment, to practice in front of a friend and receive feedback. Pay special attention to the way the body appears when contemplating the leading center and speaking with the emotional accent. A leading center should reverberate through the preacher's presence and be evident in their expression, posture, and body language. As you deliver lines accented with emotional intention, you can observe the ways that intention is spelled out in the alphabet of the flesh. The preacher can also hone expressions that need to be enhanced, diminished, or redirected.

Another element to work on during rehearsal is vocal variation. Clergy can receive different feedback on their voice, including that their language sounds lumbering and tedious. Others might be told they are too singsongy or too breathy. Some speakers make every line into a declarative statement—or worse, a question. These issues are the result of lacking vocal variation, or the principle that speech patterns must shift and change to be effective. As Alex Montoya writes in *Preaching with Passion*: "Variety includes the rate with which one speaks, sometimes rapidly as when excited, other times slow and ponderous as when deliberating or making proper use of a pause." It also includes altering the pitch one uses at the beginning and end of the sentences. Without this variety, the speech will be a monotonous drone to the congregation. The preacher can rehearse with different intentions behind the language and seek feedback about patterns they overutilize.

Finally, rehearsal can help the preacher determine which techniques and effects are helpful, and which are not. It is not expected or possible that someone will use all of the techniques explored in this chapter, but the preacher can use the ones that facilitate their own powerful delivery and discard the rest. Rehearsal is the gateway for ensuring the tools the preacher selects are the right ones.

And so, rehearse once more, with feeling.

The Dynamics of Crescendo

Passionate sermons often move toward a climax or crescendo: the finale of the sermon, the part where rhetoric and emotion are especially elevated. This technique has been around for centuries and is present in different traditions of oratory. Variations on the heightened finale can be witnessed in Pentecostal and Evangelical styles of preaching and are utilized widely by secular public speakers and political orators. Its elements are mentioned in classics such as Aristotle's *Rhetoric* and Dale Carnegie's *The Art of Public Speaking*. It is also treasured in many parts of the Black church, where speakers such as Rev. Dr. James Forbes, Prathia Hall, Rev. Dr. Otis Moss III, and Rev. Dr. William Barber II express the form deftly. The sermon culminates in a time of celebration, where the message is reinforced through rapturous emotional expression and participation. The emotional crest or crescendo is a powerful, persuasive effect that cements the message of the sermon for the gathered community.

My own approach is inspired by these diverse traditions but does not rely heavily on any one of them. I have cultivated it through trial and error, as well as reading broadly in the areas of rhetoric, speech giving, poetry, and performance. It was also inspired by my own appreciation for crescendo in music and thinking through the buildup of an emotional wave within one's body, language, and speech.

I want to emphasize that the discussion here is not an attempt to show how one can preach "just like" a particular group, tradition, or person. It is not a how-to for imitating an Evangelical pastor, political orator, or preacher in the Black church. Instead, what follows is a set of rhetorical tools that allow a preacher to identify the buildup and crest of emotion in their own body, speech, and presentation, which requires reflection on the natural elevation of one's own excitement and emotional pitch, and how to shape language to reflect that. This approach is fundamentally different from, say, mimicking the celebrative sermon in the Black church, which is theologically and sociologically distinct from other faiths. This framing is important to avoid doing a disservice to cultural traditions whose integrity and beauty could be exploited if picked apart and harvested piecemeal.

With this caution in mind, let's now turn to the dynamics of the sermon that move toward emotional crest. Many people who write about crescendo view it as a tool of message reinforcement. Speakers engage it so that, in the words of Dale Carnegie in *The Art of Public Speaking,* "the speech may rise in argument, in interest, in power, by piling one fact or appeal upon another until the climax—the highest point of influence on your audience—has been reached." Henry Mitchell argues in *Celebration & Experience in Preaching* that it reinforces the behavioral change the sermon promotes, while in *Passion in the Pulpit,* Vines and Dooley believe it enshrines the message within the heart of the preacher and the congregation. In other words, by linking the message of the sermon to a deeply felt experience just before the end, the message has a better chance of staying with the members after they leave. And at a time when distractions proliferate, preachers need to carefully consider tools that maximize attention and facilitate impact and retention.

Can one learn to create an effective crescendo? I believe the answer is yes. As I have already discussed, the preacher needs to embody the emotion that is present in the sermon. The sermon's emotional dynamics must be genuinely explored and felt both before one enters the pulpit and then during moments of intensity while preaching. Without the preacher's personal experience of the emotion, it is unlikely that the alphabet of the flesh will successfully communicate it. This is especially relevant during the crescendo, when the preacher's conviction glimmers with emotional power and intensity. The crescendo is the moment when the preacher says, "Yes, I know this much to be true. From the depths of my faith convictions, I know it. I believe it. I feel it." It is a laying-bare, an opening-up, a pouring-forth of one's feelings about the issue, whether that be lament, joy, outrage, or hope.

But how does one craft an emotional experience in oratory so that it crests and peaks? One way to think about these questions is through the dynamics of crescendo in music. Often, the music begins with a slow, quiet opening, then there is a gradual increase in pace. Perhaps more instruments are brought into the performance, or voices are slowly raised. The score becomes louder, the music faster. The increased pace and volume heighten the emotional state of the receiver. At the crescendo's peak, the emotion is at its fullest, and then the intensity of the piece begins to subside. Whether the composition provokes joy, melancholy, anxiety, etc., that emotion is mirrored in the receiver and amplified as the music rises and crests.

There are at least two lessons that translate from music to preaching. First, crescendo is, by definition, a slow rise to the peak; it is not a sudden leap from a subdued start to an exuberant climax. Likewise, for the peak of the preaching experience to make emotional sense, one needs to cultivate the emotional state in the receiver before amplifying it. The preacher cannot go from zero to ten. When people receive feedback that an emotional crest felt artificial or over-the-top, it is often because it lacked this intuitive progression. Such progression includes hints of emotional intensity in the body of the sermon, as well as the slow increase of pace.

Second, an effective crescendo does not detach from the emotional tone of a piece. If the piece is melancholy, then the crescendo will exacerbate its melancholia. If the tone is joyful, the crescendo will increase the joy. In other words, if a sermon moves from despair to hope, hope cannot be introduced at the height of the crescendo; it must be introduced before the emotional amplification and cultivated through the rise in energy and increase of pace for it to be convincing.

This buildup of emotional energy and power requires careful attention to language. First, think about what we are customarily doing when we speak with one another. Speaking to another person generally signals, *I have some information to impart to you. This is information that you may not have heard before*. Unfortunately, this assumption undermines passionate delivery at the moment of climax; passionate delivery often has a different volume and pace than conversation, both louder and faster. But if I am imparting information in an excitable voice, I will not have the effect I am hoping for. People tend to associate informational speech delivered with a loud voice as frustration or agitation. Likewise, if I start to deliver information at an increased pace, you may interpret it as nervousness. The misalignment between intention and outcome will likely kill the effect the preacher is attempting to achieve.

At the point of crescendo, it becomes necessary to tip away from the informational or explanatory and toward other linguistic frames. One way to do this is to edge into poetry, using lyrical prose to restate and reframe the message. Here, the sermon slides away from the rational and into the elliptical, away from the theological and into the theopoetic. Theopoetic language, according to Professor L. Callid Keefe-Perry in *Way to Water*, refuses mechanical statements of religious teaching in favor of experiential and intuitive truths. It relies on the surplus of meaning in imagery and symbol to generate an experience for the gathered community. When incorporated into crescendo, the poetic restatement crystallizes the message beyond argument or explanation and crafts an experience through heightened rhetoric, emotional elevation, and aphoristic verse.

Lines can shorten, becoming brief aphorisms that I sometimes call poetic ellipses. At other times, the sentences can be longer by making use of synonyms or lists broken by commas. In either case, the structure of the lines becomes less varied, which allows the preacher to develop a particular rhythm of speech. It is something like a gallop, where the energy carries from one line to the next. As the preacher builds up to this conclusion, words, phrases, and lines can be plucked from earlier in the sermon and turned into short sentences or lists. Rarely should these lines contain new information that was not embedded in the sermon, as that would return the congregation to rational processing and dilute the emotional effect of the climax. The point is to communicate emotion and passion, not information.

Below is an excerpt of one of my recent sermons, which I gave as our congregation was pursuing greater accommodations for disabled people. I preached on the theology of disability justice, pointing to the unique gifts and perspectives disability can bring. I also lifted the stories of others, using their own words to explore the concept. I attempted to reframe the issue from one where congregations barely tolerate difference to one where plurality and difference lead to a fuller concept of humanity. The sacred text was Exodus 3:8, which promises a land of milk and honey.

Here is the climax:

> I don't want to make others fit into a narrow frame. I don't want a place of belonging at the expense of our humanity, uniqueness, difference, and diversity. I don't want anxiety about fitting in or being tolerated or reducing our dimensions. I want us to arrange and rearrange, to grow and shift, to swell and expand until everyone can come. I want the frames, the limits, the boundaries to crack and open up—to open up to contours and differences, to configurations

> and variations, to widening circles and expanding limits, to multiplicity and plurality, variety and intricacy, to differences fitting into no neat set. I hunger for contrasts and divergences, for folds that unfold with no end in sight. I don't want a paradise without those. I don't want a ticket to a place without difference; I don't even want to vacation there! I want all of the layers that cluster inside and open out into complexities, contradictions, multitudes, and varieties. I want new spectrums that glimmer with color and intensity and life! I want a community that *desires* those! Because that is the milk! That is the honey! That is the land . . . that . . . has . . . been . . . promised.

In the context of the sermon, this passage restated what came before in more poetic language, which allowed for the community to sink into an emotional experience. The passage is structured so that short sentences layer one atop the other, building intensity and pace as each are spoken. The language is optimized so that I can glide from one line to the next, compounding emotional power.

As you can see from this selection, the climax does not need to be lengthy. Often, the longer this emotional language is sustained, the flatter the emotion becomes. I have heard preachers give an elevated climax for lengthy periods. For some, especially for those who are accustomed to the use of the form, this can be effective. However, for many preachers, lengthy usage may have diminishing returns. Especially if someone is newer to the use of this form and is in a context that is unfamiliar with it, the preacher can make this part as brief as thirty seconds to a minute and a half of speech. That is a small fraction of a fifteen- to twenty-minute sermon. But in my experience, the passion of even a brief moment of intensity will resonate strongly with people. It will often be the part they remember, and it will cement the message of the entire sermon.

The shorter crescendo is also a concession to cultural contexts that do not historically witness passionate expression in the pulpit. As the preacher introduces greater passion, a briefer crest can be more palatable. People will experience both the continuity of less passionate moments while witnessing a powerful and effective ending. Crescendo is also hard to sustain without congregational participation. In congregations attuned to an emotional peak, there is a circuit of energy between the preacher and the congregation; members respond with vocality and gestures, which amplify the preacher's energy. I admit that, even after preaching with emotion and passion that leads toward crescendo for years, my congregation rarely responds vocally—nor do I want that if it does not feel genuine for them. But what this means, practically, is that the passionate preacher will often have to generate the energy from their own reserves, instead of being fueled by others. For many, this means that a powerful, effective crescendo is possible, but rarely for extended lengths.

Volume

There exists a mistaken notion that passionate preaching is essentially the point in the sermon when someone starts shouting. But when emotion is expressed solely by raising one's voice, it will likely lack nuance and come across as flat. Moreover, shouting can communicate that the preacher is on the verge of losing control, which can derail the experience. During an effective crescendo, the preacher's voice will naturally be raised, but not extraordinarily so. You can practice the difference. Take a sentence and shout it. Now take a sentence and imagine that it is utterly crucial that someone hears it—if they do not hear it, something awful could befall them. Imagine sitting across the table from that person and putting that kind of emphasis on the statement. What you should notice is a slightly elevated volume. It is not a shout, but it nonetheless communicates the urgency the speaker intends.

Pace

During a crescendo, the preacher's speech will naturally speed up, communicating heightened animation and passion. However, this needs to be rehearsed so the preacher does not fall over their words. Even a moderately faster pace during this portion of the sermon will communicate the necessary emphasis. If you are worried that you might move too quickly in this portion of the sermon, or if you have received feedback that you move through your sermon too rapidly, I recommend the following practice: Take a topic that you are especially animated about, and imagine that you are communicating it to a friend with full gusto. However, as you do so, focus on enunciating *every word*. This will naturally slow you down without extinguishing the verbal fire that communicates passion.

Intonation

Some experts in using a crescendo possess a nearly singsong cadence. In *Delivering the Sermon*, Rev. Teresa Fry Brown discusses this as musicality or intonation. This is the way preachers thread their texts with lines of song—and indeed, some preachers will break into song in the middle of the sermon. (Although this is not something you will hear me do!) Luckily, singing in the middle of the sermon is not necessary to have the same effect. I like to think of intonation as what occurs when one can nearly sing a line of their text but doesn't quite do it.

To try this, think about one of the lines from "Amazing Grace"—the part that goes, "Amazing grace, how sweet the sound." First, sing that line, then reduce the musicality of the line to the point that it crosses over into a spoken word. The words should take longer to speak, and there should be more breath that surrounds them. This makes the line hover between song and spoken word, with some ambiguity about which category it belongs to. This is one way of understanding intonation, which can be part of what produces effective cadence in a sermon.

Silence

Preaching is primarily a practice of speech, but silence also has its place in preaching. The use of silence during a crescendo, in particular, can have a paradoxically amplifying effect. I think of this in terms of damming up a river: Stopping the flow causes the liquid weight to push toward its destination. In the sermon excerpt above, I used ellipses to indicate that I was elongating and slowing the final sentence, which showed there was more to come while refraining from completion. Of course, these were not extended periods of silence; they lasted no more than seconds. But the staccato effect interrupted the flow of speech in a way that increased anticipation and emphasis.

Body Language

Attending to body language and physical presence is important during the crescendo. If the preacher uses a pulpit, do they shrink away from it? Do they feel dwarfed by it? Are they in control of the space and able to use the pulpit as a tool for their expression? A good practice is to grasp the sides of the pulpit and lean in periodically, communicating comfort with the physical space. The preacher can even use this technique in place of gesture. However, if the preacher uses gesture, that also needs to be given careful consideration—during a crescendo, it is crucial that the preacher exercises control. For instance, the movement of a hand may start and end with the beginning and termination of a phrase. This smaller, briefer burst of bodily movement has a better effect than an unrestrained waving of one's arms.

Anxiety versus Excitement

Where does emotion sit in the body during the crescendo? Sometimes preachers wonder whether the elevated or excited speech of a climax will be interpreted as anxiety or agitation. They ask how the congregation will tell the difference. The answer partly has to do with refraining from informative speech in this section. The other answer has to do with the body. As discussed, our bodies transmit affect with many subtle cues that exist beyond words. Our speech also communicates these words beneath the words, and so it is important to feel the appropriate emotion and locate where it sits within the body. Some of the techniques described above, such as attending to a leading center, can assist with that.

This grounded presence should create a different felt experience from anxiety or agitation. You might spend time experimenting with this. Take an issue you care deeply about, and imagine the reasons you care about it in vivid detail. Feel that conviction and notice where it settles. Now, imagine the last time you were agitated or anxious. Feel where that sits in your body. Often, these emotions land in two different places. Commitment is experienced as deeper and more grounded, a steady center at the pit of the stomach or in the heart. Anxiety or agitation is more topsy-turvy, like a filing cabinet with everything loaded in the top drawer. When one enters the pulpit, it will be crucial to reexperience the emotion in the body. Using these techniques will make it less likely that the congregation will misread the alphabet of the flesh and experience something the preacher does not intend.

The End

Speakers who incorporate a climax have different ways of approaching the end of the sermon. Some move toward a denouement, slowing the energy and then stating a call to action. Others, upon realizing that whatever comes after the climax is anticlimactic, choose instead to "stop in the storm"—in other words, to end at the height of the emotional fervor. Here, passion is at its peak. The final line is a part of a rhapsodic wave that has swept the congregation. People are on edge, ready for more, but rather than continue, the preacher stops speaking. At this moment, it is crucial to remain firmly in the pulpit. The preacher suddenly becomes a still point while the gathered community continues to vibrate with energy. The preacher then takes a breath or sweeps their gaze over the congregation a final time. And then they quit the pulpit. The energy in the congregation begins to solidify into an emotional core that cements the message. Members are ready to leave with good news and changed hearts because, by this point, they didn't just passively receive a message, consider a few nice ideas, or sit through some fine thoughts and pretty words.

They *feel* something.

In Conclusion: Preach It!

This book has covered a lot of ground, and it can feel overwhelming to think about how all of these tips will fit together in a sermon. If you are worried, it may be helpful to remember that Rome was not built in a day. The construction of a passionate sermon is something that takes time and practice. Nonetheless, we can distill some of the advice in this book into manageable questions. The following is something of a passionate preaching checklist, which might sit next to your computer as you compose the sermon. By considering these questions while composing the message, you will have a roadmap to an effective sermon.

- Interpretation: Does my reading of the ancient text disrupt harmful interpretations? Am I offering something life-giving?
- Authority: Where in the sermon can I say, "I know this much to be true"? What is my fundamental conviction that anchors the message?
- Empathy: Have I answered the questions *why this*, *why now*, and *why this group of people*?
- Language: Is the language sensate and experiential?

- Structure: What is the problem the sermon is addressing? What is the solution? Is the movement from problem to solution compelling?
- Emotion: What is the emotional engine of the sermon? What emotion characterizes the problem, and what characterizes the solution?
- Tension: What in my sermon is keeping folks on the edge of their seats? Where do I lose the tension, and where does the energy in the sermon sag?
- Embodiment: Does my body communicate the emotions of my sermon?
- Delivery: Have I discovered and rehearsed the moments of fire and passion? Am I ready to not just preach it, but *preach* it?

A WORD OF GRATITUDE

So many people helped with this book that it is impossible to name all of them.

I appreciate my friends who talked with me into the night about these ideas, including Zackrie Vinczen, Darcy Baxter, Katie Kandarian-Morris, and Anne Clough. Kate Steinberg, Mark Pletcher, Denis Paul, Oslo Brewster, and Joe Cherry offered deep insight. The Malibu Study Group helped me sharpen a hazy first draft.

My editor, Mary Benard, and the team at Skinner House could not have been more patient and gracious. Sunshine Wolfe's insights as a sensitivity reader were invaluable.

I am indebted to my teachers and mentors, especially Mary Donovan Turner, Matthew Myer Boulton, Peter Gomes, Christina Hutchins, Kwok Pui-lan, Farid Esack, Dan McKanan, Yvette Flunder, Roger Jones, and John Buehrens. So much of what is good and beautiful in my preaching is due to their influence. The faults are mine.

In moments of discouragement, Quincy Worthington reminded me that homiletics is a worthwhile discipline and that I should keep writing. And preaching.

Bryan Cones's comments deepened the theology and depth of the project.

Ashley Theissen is friend, family, and editor. Her encouragement and feedback meant the world.

Benna Hergert, Marita Sullivan, and Scott Sullivan's support was invaluable. David and Susan Hergert always believed in my work. Jason, I wish you could read this.

Evan's love saw me through from start to finish. You hold all the pieces.

To my wonderful students at Meadville Lombard Theological School, who give me hope for the future of ministry: You inspired this project.

S.M., you gave me the words.

To the members of the North Shore Unitarian Church, who give me the privilege of their pulpit every Sunday, this book is dedicated to you.

SELECTED BIBLIOGRAPHY

Alison, Jane. *Meander, Spiral, Explode: Design and Pattern in Narrative.* Catapult, 2019.

Allen Jr., O. Wesley. *Determining the Form (Elements of Preaching).* Fortress Press, 2008.

Allen, Ronald J. (Editor). *Patterns in Preaching: A Sermon Sampler.* Des Pres: Chalice, 1998.

Aristotle. *Aristotle's Nicomachean Ethics.* Translated by Robert Bartlett and Susan Collins. University of Chicago, 2011.

Aristotle. *Rhetoric.* Translated by W. Rhys Roberts. Dover Thrift Editions, 2004.

Auden, W. H. "Funeral Blues." In *Selected Poems of W. H. Auden*, 48. Vintage, 2007.

Black, Kathy. "A Perspective of the Disabled: Transforming Images of God, Interdependence, and Healing." In *Preaching Justice: Ethnic and Cultural Perspectives*, edited by Christine Marie Smith, 6–26. Wipf and Stock, 2008.

Brennan, Teresa. *The Transmission of Affect.* Cornell University Press, 2004.

Brown, Teresa Fry. *Delivering the Sermon: Voice, Body, and Animation in Proclamation.* Fortress Press, 2008.

Brueggemann, Walter. *Finally Comes the Poet: Daring Speech for Proclamation.* Fortress Press, 1989.

Brueggemann, Walter. *The Word Militant: Preaching a Decentering Word.* Fortress Press, 2010.

Buttrick, David. *Homiletic: Moves and Structures.* Fortress Press, 1987.

Byassee, Jason. "Preaching Weird." *The Christian Century*, February 2022.

Campbell, Charles L. and Johan H. Cilliers. *Preaching Fools: The Gospel as a Rhetoric of Folly.* Baylor University Press, 2012.

Carnegie, Dale. *The Art of Public Speaking.* First Clydesdale Press, 2018.

Craddock, Fred. *As One Without Authority.* Chalice Press, 1971.

Crisp, Justin. "Introduction: A Bright Sorrow." In *Joy and Human Flourishing: Essays on Theology, Culture, and the Good Life*, edited by Miroslav Volf and Justin Crisp, vii–xviii. Fortress Press, 2015.

Cuervo, Lilia. "Response." In *Centering: Navigating Race, Authenticity, and Power in Ministry*, edited by Mitra Rahnema, 10–19. Skinner House Books, 2017.

Dykstra, Robert. "Rending the Curtain: Lament as an Act of Vulnerable Aggression." In *Lament: Reclaiming Practices in Pulpit, Pew, and Public Square*, edited by Sally A. Brown and Patrick D. Miller, 59–69. Westminster John Knox Press, 2005.

Ellis, Marc. *Toward a Jewish Theology of Liberation*. Baylor University Press, 2007.

Emerson, Ralph Waldo. "The Divinity School Address." In *Selections from Ralph Waldo Emerson*, 100–115. Edited by Stephen E. Whicher. Houghton Mifflin, 1957.

Emerson, Ralph Waldo. *The Journals and Miscellaneous Notebooks of Ralph Waldo Emerson, Volume VII: 1838–1842*. Edited by William H. Gilman. Belknap Press, 1969.

Esack, Farid. *Qur'an, Liberation and Pluralism: An Islamic Perspective of Interreligious Solidarity against Oppression*. Oneworld Publications, 1996.

Fant, Clyde E. *Preaching for Today*. New York: Harper & Row, 1977.

Ferrara, Alessandro. *Reflective Authenticity: Rethinking the Project of Modernity*. Routledge, 2002. Kindle.

Florence, Anna Carter. *Preaching as Testimony*. Westminster John Knox Press, 2007.

Gibbs, Anna. "Contagious Feelings: Pauline Hanson and the Epidemiology of Affect." *Australian Humanities Review* 24, no. 1 (2001): 1.

González, Justo. "A Hispanic Perspective: By the Rivers of Babylon." In *Preaching Justice: Ethnic and Cultural Perspectives*, 80–97. Edited by Christine Marie Smith. Wipf & Stock, 1998.

González, Justo and Catherine González. "The Neglected Interpreters." In *The Company of Preachers: Wisdom on Preaching, Augustine to the Present*, 248–264. Edited by Richard Lischer. William B. Eerdmans Publishing Company, 2002.

Harris, Scott. *An Invitation to the Sociology of Emotions*. Routledge, 2015.

Hendel, Hilary Jacobs. *It's Not Always Depression: Working the Change Triangle to Listen to the Body, Discover Core Emotions, and Connect to Your Authentic Self*. Random House, 2018.

Hergert, Lucas. "Under the Preacher's Robes: A Queer Embodied Homiletic." In *Queering Christian Worship: Reconstructing Liturgical Theology*, edited by Bryan Cones, Sharon R. Fennema, W. Scott Haldeman, and Stephen Burns, 143–152. Seabury Books, 2023.

Herzog, William. *Parables as Subversive Speech: Jesus as Pedagogue of the Oppressed.* Westminster John Knox Press, 1994.

Hochschild, Arlie. *The Managed Heart: Commercialization of Human Feeling.* University of California Press, 2012.

Horsley, Richard A. *Jesus and the Powers: Conflict, Covenant, and Hope for the Poor.* Fortress Press, 2010.

Jackson, Darrick. "Othering and Belonging." In *Centering: Navigating Race, Authenticity, and Power in Ministry*, edited by Mitra Rahnema, 1–9. Skinner House Books, 2017.

Jaggar, Alison. "Love and Knowledge: Emotions in Feminist Epistemology." *Inquiry* 32, no. 2 (1989): 151–176.

James, William. *A Pluralistic Universe.* Harvard University Press, 1977.

Keefe-Perry, L. Callid (2014). *Way to Water: A Theopoetics Primer.* Cascade.

Kim, Eunjoo Mary. "Responses." In *The Renewed Homiletic*, edited by O. Wesley Allen, 100–104. Fortress Press, 2010.

LaRue, Cleophus. *Rethinking Celebration: From Rhetoric to Praise in African American Preaching.* Westminster John Knox Press, 2016.

LaRue, Cleophus. "Two Ships Passing in The Night." In *What's the Matter with Preaching Today?* edited by Mike Graves, 127–144. Westminster John Knox Press, 2004.

Long, Thomas G. and Cornelius Plantinga (Editors). *A Chorus of Witnesses: Model Sermons for Today's Preacher.* William B. Eerdmans Publishing Company, 1994.

Lowry, Eugene. *The Homiletical Plot: The Sermon as Narrative Art Form.* Westminster John Knox Press, 1980.

Lowry, Eugene. *The Homiletical Beat: Why All Sermons Are Narrative.* Abingdon Press, 2012.

McClure, John (Editor). *Best Advice for Preaching.* Fortress Press, 1998.

Mitchell, Henry. *Celebration & Experience in Preaching.* Abingdon Press, 2008.

Mitchell, Henry. "Celebration Renewed." In *The Renewed Homiletic*, edited by O. Wesley Allen, 63–73. Fortress Press, 2010.

Montoya, Alex. *Preaching with Passion.* Kregel Publications, 2007.

Moss III, Otis. *Blue Note Preaching in a Post-Soul World: Finding Hope in an Age of Despair.* Westminster John Knox Press, 2015.

Muñoz, José. *Cruising Utopia: The Then and There of Queer Futurity.* NYU Press, 2009.

Nussbaum, Martha. *Upheavals of Thought: The Intelligence of Emotions.* Cambridge University Press, 2001.

Nye, Naomi Shihab. "So Much Happiness." In *Words Under the Words: Selected Poems*, 88. The Eighth Mountain Press, 1994.

Rankin, David. "From the Masthead to the Hatches: The Sources of Authority in the Liberal Pulpit." In *Transforming Words: Six Essays on Preaching*, edited by William Schulz, 2–14. Skinner House Books, 1984.

Reid, Robert Stephen. *The Four Voices of Preaching: Connecting Purpose and Identity behind the Pulpit.* Brazos Press, 2006.

Ripley, Ezra. "Changes in Religious Opinions and the Character of Preaching in New England during the Last Fifty Years." Unitarian Universalist Ministers Association. https://uuma.org/berry-street-essay/bse1830/.

Robinson, Charles. "Alleged Defects of Unitarian Preaching." Unitarian Universalist Ministers Association. https://uuma.org/berry-street-essay/bse1844/.

Rumi, Jalal al-Din Muhammad. "Birdwings." In *The Essential Rumi*, 174. Translated by Coleman Barks and John Moyne. HarperOne, 2004.

Sanders, Cheryl. "Preaching with Passion." In *Power in the Pulpit: How America's Most Effective Black Preachers Prepare Their Sermons*, edited by Cleophus LaRue, 117–132. Westminster John Knox Press, 2002.

Schmemann, Alexander. *The Journals of Father Alexander Schmemann 1973–1983.* Translated by Juliana Schmemann. St. Vladimir's Seminary Press, 2000.

Schneider, Laurel and Thelathia Young. *Queer Soul and Queer Theology: Ethics and Redemption in Real Life.* Routledge, 2021.

Schüssler Fiorenza, Elisabeth. *The Power of the Word: Scripture and the Rhetoric of Empire.* Fortress Press, 2007.

Shuster, Marguerite. "The Truth and Truthfulness: Theological Reflections on Preaching and Performance." In *Performance in Preaching: Bringing the Sermon to Life*, edited by Jana Childers and Clayton Schmit, 20–43. Baker Academic, 2008.

Schweitzer, Albert. *The Quest of the Historical Jesus.* Translated by W. Montgomery. Adam and Charles Black, 1911.

Seneca, Lucius Annaeus. *On Anger.* Translated by Aubrey Stewart. Montecristo Publishing, 2020. Kindle.

Smith, Christine M. *Weaving the Sermon: Preaching in a Feminist Perspective.* Westminster John Knox Press, 1989.

Smith, James K. A. *Desiring the Kingdom: Worship, Worldview, and Cultural Formation.* Baker Academic, 2009.

Spurgeon, Charles Haddon. *Lectures to My Students.* Hendrickson Publishing Group, 2010.

Strawn, Brent A. *Honest to God Preaching: Talking Sin, Suffering, and Violence.* Fortress Press, 2021.

Subraman, Belinda. "Book Passion." *Steam Ticket,* VII (2004).

Taylor, Barbara Brown. "Preaching." In *The Company of Preachers,* edited by Richard Lischer, 46–57. William B. Eerdmans Publishing Company, 2002.

Thomas, Frank A. *How to Preach a Dangerous Sermon.* Abingdon Press, 2018.

Thomas, Frank A. *They Like to Never Quit Praisin' God: The Role of Celebration in Preaching.* Pilgrim Press, 2013.

Thompson, Lisa. *Ingenuity: Preaching as an Outsider.* Abingdon Press, 2018.

Tisdale, Leonora Tubbs. *How Women Transform Preaching.* Abingdon Press, 2021.

Townes, Emilie. *Womanist Ethics and the Cultural Production of Evil.* Palgrave MacMillan, 2007.

Turner, William C. "The Musicality of Black Preaching: Performing the Word." *Performance in Preaching: Bringing the Sermon to Life,* edited by Jana Childers and Clayton Schmit (260–286). Baker Academic, 2008.

Vines, Jerry and Adam Dooley. *Passion in the Pulpit: How to Exegete the Emotion of Scripture.* Moody Publishers, 2018.

Walker, James. "Real and Alleged Defects of Unitarian Preaching." Unitarian Universalist Ministers Association. https://uuma.org/berry-street-essay/bse1836/.

Walker, Nathan. *Exorcising Preaching: Crafting Intellectually Honest Worship.* Chalice Press, 2014.

Ward, David. *Practicing the Preaching Life.* Abingdon Press, 2019.

Yeats, W. B. "The Second Coming." In *The Collected Works of W. B. Yeats, Vol. 1: The Poems,* edited by Richard J. Finneran, 200. Scribner, 1997.